Leadership Literacy

Leadership Literacy
The Solution to Our Present Crisis

By

Daniel S. Clemens

LEADERSHIP
AMERICA

Englewood, Colorado

Leadership Literacy: The Solution to Our Present Crisis

Copyright © 1992 by Daniel S. Clemens

PRINTED IN THE UNITED STATES OF AMERICA

10   9   8   7   6   5   4   3   2   1

ISBN   0-9632640-7-9
Library of Congress Catalog Number   92-81806

Book Cover Design and Watercolor Illustration
by
Peggy Ann Goold

Grateful acknowledgement is made for permission to reprint exerpts from the following copyrighted material:

Cultural Literacy by E.D. Hirsch. Copyright © 1987 by Houghton Mifflin, Company. All rights reserved.; Reprinted by permission of The Putnam Publishing Group from *Plain Speaking* by Merle Miller. Copyright © 1973, 1974 by Merle Miller.; Reprinted by permission of: Joan Daves Agency. Copyright © 1958 by Martin Luther King, Jr.,1963 by Martin Luther King, Jr., renewed by Coretta Scott King 1991,1961 by Martin Luther King, Jr., 1963 by Martin Luther King, Jr., renewed by Coretta Scott King 1991, 1968 by The Estate of Martin Luther King, Jr.; *Voices of Freedom* ed. by Henry Hampton and Steve Fayer. Copyright © 1990 by Blackside. Permission granted by Bantam Books.;*Robert F. Kennedy: In His Own Words* ed. by Edwin O. Guthman and Jeffrey Shulman. Copyright © 1988 by Robert F. Kennedy Memorial. Permission granted by Bantam Books.;*Leaders* by Warren Bennis and Burt Nanus. Copyright © 1985 by Warren Bennis and Burt Nanus. Permission granted by HarperCollins Publishers.; *Kennedy* by Theodore C. Sorensen. Copyright © 1965 by Theodore C. Sorensen. Permission granted by HarperCollins Publishers.; Reprinted by permission of Warner Books from *Leaders* © Copyright 1982 by Richard Nixon.; Kouzes, J.M., and B.Z. Posner. *The Leadership Challenge: How to Get Extraordinary Things Done in Organizations.* San Francisco: Jossey-Bass Inc., Publishers, 1987.; Thirteen Days by Robert F. Kennedy. Copyright © 1969 by W. W. Norton & Co, Inc.; *A Moment in History* by Brent Ashabranner. Copyright © 1971 by Brent Ashabranner. Reprinted by permission of the author.; *A Nation of Immigrants* by John F. Kennedy. Copyright © 1963 by Anti-Defamation League of B'nia Brith. Permission granted by HarperCollins Publishers.

Grateful acknowledgement is also made to THE UPI/BETTMANN ARCHIVE for artist reference photos for cover design of Lee Iacocca, Harry Truman and Martin Luther King, Jr.

Table of Contents

Acknowledgements

Introduction   1

1.   Susan B. Anthony   11
         Failure is Impossible
         The Way She Did Business

2.   Harry S. Truman   45
         The Truman Committee
         End of War, Trouble Begins
         The Korean Decisions

3.   John F. Kennedy   88
         The Torch is Passed
         Growth of a Leader

4.   Lee Iacocca   136
         The Ford Years
         Trying Times at Chrysler

5.   Martin Luther King, Jr.   159
         The Dream
         We Shall Overcome

      The Challenge   206

      Index   211

Acknowledgements

Writing this book was something I felt deeply and strongly that I had to do. It was my "Field of Dreams." Similar to Ray Kinsella (the main character of the 1989 movie, *Field of Dreams*, played by Kevin Costner), I too, heard voices urging me to act on a dream. These "voices," however, were not mysterious and unspecific—they were the kind words of support and encouragement of my family and friends.

I'd like to thank my close friends, Shaun Loewen, Jannine Mohr, Mark Haney, Mike Best, Brian Eisenach and Kyle Taylor for their belief in me and this project.

My thanks goes to Amy Overland and Dave Jones who offered invaluable advice and whose counsel helped me express my ideas in a more clear, efficient and effective manner.

Throughout the writing process, I have benefitted greatly from a very special group—I greatly appreciate the support of my wife's family, Dick, Betty, Dave and Irene Boydstun.

I also gratefully acknowledge the encouragement of my family. My grandparents, John and Marion Clemens and Ursula Pavola (May 28, 1901—December 26, 1991) have been a great source of inspiration and helped fuel my drive to succeed. My parents, Phil and Jan, and sister, Laurie, have consistently given me the emotional support necessary for the completion of this project. They generously furnished me with encouragement and advice—it was their faith in me that helped transform *Leadership Literacy* from dream into reality.

First, and foremost, however, I acknowledge the sacrifice and assistance of my wife Beverly. While I stayed at home and wrote each day, she supported the two of us financially for two years on, believe it or not, a teacher's salary. She helped me develop many of the ideas in the book by giving honest, insightful and objective opinions after reading its many different drafts. Without her strength, love and support, I could not have completed the book.

To America's leadership . . .

present and future

Dave:
Your strength of vision is not only inspirational and an excellent model to learn from, but it is also an essential leadership characteristic that all too many overlook. Watching you lead and shape the magazine has been an exciting and valuable lesson in leadership. I wish you continued success in leadership — your magazine, and ultimately your country, need you!

A MAN CAN BE STRONG AND STILL LIKE ROSES

Enjoy -

Dail S. Clemens

Introduction

Who Are Society's Leaders?

Throughout time humans have sought those who could lead—people who could cultivate an environment in which we would have the opportunity to be properly housed and fed, to be safe from aggression, to be emotionally and spiritually fulfilled, and to have the freedom to be individuals. The function of a leader has been to improve the environment in which his or her people live. The American Founding Fathers had much of this in mind when they wrote the Constitution. Although they were unable to imagine society's growth to its present vast, diverse and complex state, their document made possible the emergence of the United States as an economic, technological, militaristic and social superpower.

However, one vital prerequisite for success the Founding Fathers could not provide to future generations was leadership. Fortunately Washington, Jefferson, Lincoln and the Roosevelts exercised exceptional leadership at pivotal times in American history. But their successes would be less significant without the contributions of the many thousands of less visible leaders of the past two centuries. While the Constitution made it possible, these men and women created a United States that has enjoyed greatness in the twentieth century.

As we prepare to enter the twenty-first century, American dominance is eroding. The fundamental reason for this decline is that recent generations have been unable to develop the important ingredient for success that the Founding Fathers could not bequeath us—leadership.

We have become apathetic toward leadership by ignoring the importance of filling society's leadership positions with qualified leaders. Too often we dismiss leadership as someone else's responsibility. The importance of leadership and its inherent role in our society can be explained through a unique analogy.

The federal government acts as a large net, catching many of the larger problems and challenges facing the United States. Under this wide net are tighter-meshed state governmental nets which filter out some of the smaller and regional problems that escape the larger holes of the federal net. Below the states' nets are the local governmental nets which catch the smaller and localized problems not snagged by the states. All problems not caught by one of these nets fall to the ground where the individual is forced to deal with them. National defense is an issue large enough to be caught by the federal net, but an issue such as public education falls through and becomes the responsibility of the states. Real estate zoning codes fall through both nets and are caught by the local governments. However, each net is not without flaws. Our system begins to struggle when some of the larger problems escape the higher net and form a pile on the lower. The resultant strain is visible in health care, agriculture, Social Security, crime and most social programs. In these cases, the lower nets and ultimately, the individual must assume a portion of the responsibility, or the system fails. Recently the governmental nets have become worn and frayed and if not repaired, the individual in society will become over-burdened. Incompetent people within the system create the strain on the nets— this makes leadership so important. Only through good, strong leadership can America repair the nets and redistribute the load appropriately throughout the levels of society.

When functioning smoothly, our system of nets exemplifies a model form of society. In an ideal socialist state, almost nothing would escape the nets, but the public loses certain freedoms and is responsible for paying high taxes. Nothing is done in a fascist state unless the one person in charge believes it to be necessary. In an anarchical state there are no nets. This forces the society to regress to the law of the jungle where the individual is responsible for everything. We often forget how fortunate we are.

We do not need to reinvent our system of nets. Rather, our task is two-pronged: first to solve the problems that have fallen to the ground by escaping the flawed nets, and second to repair the nets and redistribute the load appropriately throughout the levels of society.

When the nets do not adequately filter problems and challenges we must organize society, with or without the assistance of government, to solve them. Although politicians are an integral component of America's leadership, we must not overlook the importance of small business owners, coaches, account executives, scout masters, educators, store managers and law enforcers. Their daily decisions can and do significantly impact the lives of others. It is their characters and actions, in concert with or in spite of government, which form American culture and which gives the United States its power.

For example, the function of a high school basketball coach is not only to win, but to facilitate the learning and enjoyment of the sport for the participants. But a leader in this role expands on this function; she is concerned with winning, but for the betterment of society, she tries to improve her players as human beings. She teaches them about life as she teaches them about basketball. As a leader in society, she also seizes many opportunities in her role as a high school coach to improve her school and community. The leadership she exhibits can compensate for shortfalls in other areas of society.

This same type of leadership is evident in the owner of a small business who organizes a program for the local restaurants to donate their leftover food each night to the needy and the homeless, by the school teacher who instructs reading and writing to the illiterate once a week, by the police officer who develops neighborhood watch programs in his spare time, and by the office manager who organizes a recycling program in her office. Each of these people are true American leaders because they give their time and energy to help lighten the load on society caused by its flawed netting. Thus, by each of us becoming a better leader, we can channel the problems that initially escaped the nets back through the system to be filtered by the appropriate net.

But if we do not address the flawed netting itself, the problems we solve for the short term will continue to plague society over the long term. It is the responsibility of our elected and appointed officials to repair and maintain the system of governmental nets. However, it is our responsibility as an electorate and constituency to choose the best persons for these positions. Our emphasis should be to develop, educate and encourage our country's most capable citizens to fill society's traditional leadership positions. Therefore, every American, whether or not he or she makes the conscious decision to become one of society's leaders, MUST have an understanding of what leadership is.

Leadership Literacy

In his best-selling work *Cultural Literacy*, E. D. Hirsch, Jr. explains that Americans are in danger of becoming culturally illiterate. He defines cultural literacy as having "the basic information needed to thrive in the modern world." Hirsch contends that to be a culturally literate person, one needs to have a basic understanding of history, the sciences, literature, civics, music, art—the specific components that make our culture uniquely American. This fundamental knowledge, says Hirsch, is the common thread that holds America together by fostering "effective nationwide communication." He maintains that if strangers possess a certain amount of common knowledge "their communications can be short and efficient, subtle and complex. But if strangers share very little knowledge, their communications must be long and relatively rudimentary." He asserts that if the American population became more culturally literate, it could help to lessen the sectional differences developing in the United States. Furthermore, cultural literacy "enables grandparents to communicate with grandchildren, Southerners with Midwesterners, whites with blacks, Asians with Hispanics, and Republicans with Democrats."

The concept of leadership literacy is similar to Hirsch's idea of cultural literacy. Because leadership is vital to the success of our nation, there are certain people, events and personal leadership characteristics that every American needs to know and understand. With just a rudimentary understanding of leadership, society is only capable of scratching the surface in a meaningful discussion of its current leadership status.

The goal of this book is help the reader attain basic literacy in leadership. A leadership literate person understands the concept and importance of leadership, understands the essential five personal characteristics for effective leadership, can identify these characteristics in others, can apply them to his or her own life, can differentiate between leadership and management, and understands what exactly made key historical figures great leaders.

Leadership Defined

Given that we need good leaders to solve our problems, we need to know exactly what we mean when we say leadership. Leadership is **the process of establishing a meaningful long-term goal and organizing the efforts of those who share the goal, so that their individual talents and abilities may be put to their best use**.

Leadership is absolutely dependent on a long-term goal—a vision. James Kouzes and Barry Posner define a vision as "an ideal and unique image of the future." Warren Bennis and Burt Nanus explain that "a vision articulates a view of a realistic, credible attractive future for the organization, a condition that is better in some important ways than now exists." But the importance of a vision for a leader is the affect it has upon the followers. Kouzes and Posner's research found that:

> . . . a clear vision is a powerful force. It has significant influence on followers. When leaders clearly articulated their vision for the organization, people reported significantly higher levels of job satisfaction, commitment, loyalty, esprit de corps, clarity of direction,

> pride and productivity. It is quite evident that clearly articulated visions make a difference.

In short, a vision gives the leader and followers purpose, focus and motivation.

Without a vision, the present situation cannot be put into context. If the future cannot be made better in some important way, then there is no reason to leave the present. Therefore, without a vision, there is no reason to act, and without a need for action, there is no need for leadership. Thus, the defining aspect of leadership is vision.

We often confuse management with leadership; they are not synonyms nor are they interchangeable concepts. A manager, by definition, is a person hired to direct and control a portion of an organization to achieve a pre-determined objective. A manager maintains the status quo and executes within the existing system, while a leader creates and defines the system itself. Vision is the one personal characteristic that separates leaders from managers. This important management-leadership distinction is also illustrated by the manner in which the success of each is judged—a good manager is *efficient*; a good leader is *effective*.

Using a car as an example, management would constitute the dashboard and control panels. These important parts of the car monitor the speed, engine temperature, transmission, cooling system, electrical system and control the interior climate conditions. In this same model, leadership is composed of the steering wheel, brake and gas pedals, clutch and gear shift, turn signals and headlights. While management controls and monitors the efficiency and performance of the car, leadership, with the ability to change direction and speed depending on the road ahead, is responsible for the car effectively reaching the proper destination.

Without leadership, no organization, regardless of how efficient the management, can survive, let alone thrive in our rapidly changing capitalistic society. Certainly our nation, with its vast and complex social and economic problems, cannot thrive without strong, effective leadership. Management, however, is vitally important. Without efficient people to execute decisions, organize programs and share in the workload, a leader's vision, regardless of how attractive, will not be realized. To meet the challenges and problems facing the United States, we must ask more of our leaders—they must be both efficient and effective.

In addition to vision, there are four other characteristics that make a leader truly exceptional. First, a leader must have integrity. Establishing sound moral principles and operating with honesty lay the foundation for integrity. While trust and using power wisely are important, a leader must build integrity through thought, words and action. A leader must earn credibility and respect. Former President Harry S. Truman emphasized the importance of integrity in a leader: "I don't think knowing what's the right thing to do ever gives anybody much trouble. It's *doing* the right thing that seems to give a lot of people trouble."

Second, a leader must be decisive. This is a three step process: Perspective—Foresight—Execution. For a leader to make good decisions, he or she must thoroughly understand the problem. Only by studying the past and present of the situation can the leader form a valid perspective. Then he or she must use foresight to predict the results and consequences of the many possible courses of action. Once the leader decides, he or she executes it through the proper channels using protocol appropriate for the situation. To be decisive, a leader must have a thorough understanding of how the past and present will relate to the future.

Third, a leader must be able to communicate effectively. Public speaking can be an important part of many leadership positions, but it is only a portion of being a successful communicator. Another portion consists of strong interpersonal skills. The final, and perhaps most vital portion is striking a balance between listening and speaking. Placing equal importance on upward and downward communication, a leader will design his or her organization to foster the smooth exchange of thoughts and ideas. Without communication, confusion, rumor, frustration and inaction stifle the group's efforts.

The final essential leadership quality is resiliency. How a leader handles adversity is a litmus test of his or her leadership ability. Because adversity is a part of life, a good leader possesses the mental toughness to learn and grow from mistakes and setbacks.

This is by no means a complete list of the personal characteristics necessary for a leader to possess, but it is a strong foundation upon which a successful leader will build. Further personalizing a leader's style are the beliefs, experiences and knowledge accumulated throughout life. In the same way they make a person unique, they give a leader's style a distinct personality. Thus, we lead from our own life experiences. To create our leadership literate society, we not only must be able to recognize these five vital attributes in others, but we must help our leaders develop them.

The Present Crisis

We have all been witness to examples of poor leadership in our everyday routines. But these "small" instances are symptoms of a larger problem of a leadership illiterate society. When news directors present the public with a biased account of the day's events, our media has failed. When our schools graduate students without giving them the basic skills necessary to be productive members of society, our educational system has failed. When politicians fail to balance the welfare of the nation with that of their community, our government has failed. These failures rightfully spark a general discontent with the public, and the public in turn, shows less and less confidence in the leadership. Without public confidence, the leadership concentrates less on finding and executing solutions to the problems and concentrates more on absolving themselves from the previous failures. Soon, the leadership is preoccupied solely with laying blame while the system becomes so tangled with mistrust that it nearly ceases to function.

Politics is teeming with blame and mistrust. Although our two-party system has many benefits, a major flaw has developed. Both Democrats and Republicans concern themselves with condemning the other party and "tattling" to the public, "I told you so." This prevents any daring contemporary politician, fearing retribution and public humiliation, from taking a political risk and making the tough decisions. Consequently, those in government today spend their time constructing a good defense rather than creating an offense to solve this country's problems. This is not leadership—it is damage control.

Damage control prevents America's leaders from finding effective solutions. An effective solution, one that will work for the short and long term, will be balanced between idealism and realism. Solutions tilted too far to the side of idealism may be impractical and fail miserably because we do not live in an ideal world. However, if the tilt is too far to the realistic side, creativity is overlooked and the solution is a stale assembly of old ideas. The stereotypical Democrat tends to approach problem solving from the perspective of how the world should function under ideal conditions. But we do not live in an ideal world, and often these idealistic solutions, although rooted in goodwill, create more problems when implemented in our imperfect world. The stereotypical Republican simply observes what was done in the past and makes minor adjustments to keep it functioning. The result of the traditional merging of these two viewpoints is a program containing the negative characteristics of each—it is benign quick-fix for the short term which neither works nor offends anyone.

Damage control also is highly visible in the methods our leaders have used with other current problems: wide-spread drug abuse, a fraying educational system, overcrowded prisons, stiff foreign competition in the marketplace, racial prejudice, an unsettled Eastern Europe and Middle East, and a deteriorating natural environment. These problems indicate an obvious lack of good leadership at many levels of our society. This "leadership void" has not only had adverse effects upon the present—the absence of leaders as positive role models has stunted the leadership growth of American youth for nearly three decades. Because this trickle-down approach to leadership training is obviously not working, we are in

dire need of a trickle-up approach. Creating a leadership literate
society must be at the core of a trickle-up strategy.

The Quest

Many recent books have explored the theoretical aspects of
leadership. But we humans find the study of personalities much
more interesting and appealing than theory. For example, in the
study of psychology we prefer to read about a specific case of a
multiple personality, Sibyl for instance, to a dry explanation of the
theory and definitions of multiple personality disorder. For this
reason, I have decided to set theory aside and employ a more
vivisectional approach to the study of leadership. This book profiles
five men and women who have effectively handled the problems or
obstacles they faced; inspired others to follow their causes; were
consistently looked to for advice, opinion and direction; and made
contributions to society that changed the way Americans viewed the
world.

No two historians could reach consensus upon the best
American leaders of the last 125 years. I don't claim my selections
to be that period's best. I do claim that the character they displayed
throughout their lives makes them excellent role models from which
to study leadership and begin the trickle-up process. Whether or not
we agree with their goals, causes or politics is of no consequence. I
ask the reader to look past the politics of each situation and focus on
the leadership that each leader exhibited. It is not my purpose to
defend or condemn the decisions that were made—we learn more
about leadership from the processes than from the results.

Leadership is not bound by race, gender, political affiliation,
age or time. To solve the multitude and diverseness of our current
problems, Americans must find and employ leaders exhibiting the
decisiveness and integrity of Harry S. Truman, blessed with the
communicative and visionary brilliance of John Kennedy and Martin
Luther King, Jr. and armed with the determination and resiliency of
Susan B. Anthony and Lee Iacocca. Such leaders exist. Let our
search begin . . .

Chapter 1

Susan B. Anthony

Very few men or women have given as much of their lives and of their person to any cause as Susan B. Anthony did for woman's rights. She spent most of her adult life working to give women the right to vote; for 50 years she suffered the slings and arrows of a male-dominated establishment that, for a variety of reasons, denied women the ballot. Anthony's style of leadership— visionary with a blend of high ethical standards and a stalwart resiliency—made it possible for women to make progress as they waded upstream against a strong current of opposition. Women and minorities are still advancing on this journey upstream in America, but Anthony's leadership through some difficult rapids carried humankind closer to the headwaters that we will eventually reach— the realization and practice that all men and women are created equal.

To properly understand the amount of courage and determination that was needed by Anthony to continue her struggle for gender equality, it is necessary to explain the societal norms and belief structure of nineteenth century America. It was socially unacceptable for women to speak in public or to involve themselves in social issues. They were expected to stay in the home, cooking, cleaning, sewing and taking care of their large families. The belief that women were inherently inferior to men was widely-held by members of both sexes. Laws varied from state to state, but generally married women were not legally able to own property. Even the money women made from cooking or sewing belonged to the husband. In a divorce, all children belonged solely to the husband. If her husband beat her, a woman was rarely able to bring legal action against him. Men commonly earned 10 times the amount as women for the same job and, although women were permitted to hold public office, they were unable to vote. Colleges and universities refused enrollment to women, and girls were fortunate if they were taught more math than multiplication tables in grade school. Slavery was thriving in the United States and women had only a few more legal rights than the slave. This was the mind-set of the nation that Susan B. Anthony had to change before gender equality could be attained.

The Anthonys were a prominent Quaker family in Adams, Massachusetts. Susan's parents came from diverse backgrounds. Daniel Anthony's Quaker sect—the Society of Friends—frowned on his decision to marry his sweetheart, Lucy Read, a jovial and lively girl from a Baptist family. Quakers had to conform to strict dress, language and thought codes and all major independent actions had to be approved by the congregation. Lucy appeased the Anthony family, and to a lesser degree the Society of Friends, by converting to the Quaker lifestyle, but lost in her new way of life were her colorful dresses, beautiful singing voice and her love for dancing.

Susan Brownell Anthony, Daniel and Lucy's second child, was born on February 15, 1820. Susan was blessed with a sharp intellect and learned to read and write before the age of five. While Susan was six, the family moved to Battenville, New York as her father became managing partner of a cotton factory owned by John McLean. In addition to the factory, the two men built a general store to sell their goods and a boarding house for their unmarried workers. Business thrived, which allowed Daniel to send Susan and her older sister, Guelma, to a private school near Philadelphia. Susan's thirst for knowledge led to frequent altercations with school master Deborah Moulson. The curriculum focused on "The Principles of Morality, Humility and the Love of Virtue." Because all letters were censored by Moulson, Susan confided in her diary that she did not have the opportunity to learn what she was interested in. While she yearned for assignments in math and science, she was being taught lessons on etiquette and social grace. At that time few schools offered math and science to women.

The Anthonys' adherence to the Quaker beliefs and lifestyle changed over time. Daniel was always a progressive thinker and often crossed the line of tolerance granted by the Society of Friends.

Lucy encouraged the children to enjoy themselves but also to obey the rules of the Society. The Anthonys had frequent disputes with the sect's decisions and later left the Society. Susan held many of the fundamental beliefs and principles of Quaker thought throughout her life, but over time she disregarded the bulk of the rigid rules of the religion. She enjoyed colorful dress, independent thinking, a sense of humor and occasional minor mischief.

The troubled economic times during the panic of 1838, caused by President Andrew Jackson destroying the Federal Bank, resulted in financial woes for most Americans including the Anthonys. To make ends meet Susan took a teaching job in New Rochelle, New York. She tried many other money making ventures including silkworm cultivation, selling homemade crafts and even being a governess for a wealthy Fort Edward family. In early 1843 her Uncle Joshua Read offered Susan a position as the principal of the girls department at the coeducational Canajoharie (New York) Academy, of which he was a trustee. Susan enjoyed the job and displayed a breadth of knowledge and such a skill for teaching that she was labeled "the smartest woman in Canajoharie." But salary was not commensurate with ability at the Academy. Although she was making more money than she ever had, it was still many times less than earned by her male counterparts. Her salary did, however, afford her a comfortable lifestyle and many fine clothes which she loved to wear.

In 1848 her cousin Margaret, with whom she had been living while teaching in Canajoharie, died from complications during childbirth. Having reached the top of her payscale and having achieved the most any woman could aspire to in Canajoharie, Anthony looked for other interests to occupy her time. Although she frequently dated, she declined several marriage proposals because her suitors were either too childish or drank excessively. Anthony thought of traveling to California the next spring to strike it rich in the gold rush but in the summer of 1848 a landmark event in the history of woman's rights took place in Seneca Falls, New York that would inspire a lifetime of commitment from the young lady.

The Seneca Falls Woman's Rights Convention of July 1848 was the first gathering of women to discuss and voice their displeasure with the legal and political treatment of their gender. Lucretia Mott and Elizabeth Cady Stanton organized the Convention and since neither woman knew the rules of order, James Mott, Lucretia's husband, presided over the affair. The first day opened with speeches, discussion and debate concerning several woman's issues with only women in attendance. On the second day many men attended the event including ex-slave Frederick Douglass. Cady Stanton read her Declaration of Sentiments, a revised version of the Declaration of Independence. Her document condemned the injustices of the American system toward women in much the same way Jefferson's masterpiece denounced the British throne's tyranny of the previous century.

The event received national attention, but most newspapers scoffed at it referring to it as "the hen convention." The convention had a profound affect on the Anthony family. Susan enthusiastically read the reports and was excited by the resolutions passed there: better opportunities for women in work and education, the right to own property, the right to free public speech and equal pay for equal work. These radical ideas made sense to Anthony as women in Quaker families enjoyed a more active role in their society's decision making process than the average woman of the nineteenth century. Susan was pleased to learn that her entire family had attended the second woman's rights convention two weeks later in Rochester, New York. Surprising to Susan was that her family had signed the petitions that included a resolution for woman suffrage—Quakers did not vote as they believed it wrong to support any government that would participate in war. It was Susan B. Anthony's personal interest in the convention and enthusiastic family support that channeled her efforts into public life.

In harmony with her Quaker beliefs, the temperance crusade was the first social reform issue that Anthony became involved in. Believing that the enfranchisement of women into the system would speed the reform process, she began her own crusade for woman suffrage. She spent the remaining 56 years of her life fighting for social reforms and the equal treatment of women by the American government. Susan B. Anthony died in 1906 prior to witnessing her five decades of ceaseless work grow into fruition. The Nineteenth Amendment to the Constitution granting women the right to vote was ratified in 1920.

Although the movement actually began with the spark at Seneca Falls, Anthony played decisive roles in formative stages of the cause and later in its progression through the many difficult times. Many women and men can claim a partial responsibility for the success of the movement, but Anthony did everything that needed to be done—and more. She was given and/or assumed the responsibility as the fund-raiser, the coordinator, the accountant, the promoter, the speech writer, the decision maker, the strategist, the campaigner, and the motivator—a real "Jane" of all trades. Her vision, resilient character, will to succeed, and ability to determine and execute the multitude of necessary tasks made her the guiding force, and prompted one observer to affectionately label her the "Napoleon" of the movement. Her warm personality and high ethical standards won her the admiration of both supporters and opponents. Susan B. Anthony, having no role model to guide her, was, and continues to be, an inspiration and a role model of effective leadership for those believing in a cause.

FAILURE IS IMPOSSIBLE

Although it would prove to be a monumental task, Susan B. Anthony's vision was relatively simple. Her ideal and unique image of the future was to create an America where women would enjoy economic, social and political equality with men. This vision was the pervasive ingredient of all her endeavors and it provided her, and those involved in the movement, with purpose, focus and motivation. This vision gave her the strength to show resiliency in the face of the many and frequent disappointments she and her cause would suffer.

In essence, Anthony was a saleswoman—she was selling the goals and ideals of the woman's movement to a skeptical and frequently hostile American nation. All successful salespeople will affirm that being told "no" should not be taken personally, that a negative response is part of the business. But the "no's" Susan B. Anthony and the other activists received often were personal. The belief structure and mind-set of nineteenth century America heavily taxed her determination, stamina, will and character. For more than five decades Anthony and other reformers displayed a magnificent resiliency to endure the perpetual mental and emotional abuse. Although the setbacks and insults were too abundant and frequent to count, there were four significant events which changed the direction of the woman's movement: The 1852-53 Conventions, The Civil War, The Kansas Campaign and Susan B. Anthony's arrest and indictment for illegal voting.

Anthony's efforts during these gloomy times kept the movement alive and made possible the ultimate realization of its goals. Her optimistic and often repeated belief, "failure is impossible" was not only an accurate description of Anthony's will but it became a symbol of the movement as it neared the turn of the century. Susan B. Anthony's lifetime of determination and her resilient character are testimony to the strength of the human spirit.

The 1852-53 Conventions

Susan B. Anthony first became involved in social issues by joining the Daughters of Temperance, a sister organization of the Sons of Temperance which, as all men's organizations of the time, was open only to men. Temperance societies had become quite popular by the mid-nineteenth century as many members believed that the United States had become a nation of drinkers. They further believed that the nation's willingness to tip the bottle was having adverse affects on the family institution and the moral fabric of the nation. Anthony's zeal and competence as an activist for this cause pumped vitality into the Canajoharie, New York branch of the Daughters of Temperance, her hometown chapter. The visionary

Anthony believed that the greatest good could be achieved if her organization could pool its resources and unite with the Sons of Temperance.

In 1851 she began to organize new branches of the Daughters in neighboring towns with the hope that they could soon join the Sons. As she was still a teacher in Canajoharie, this work required most of her free time on weekends and holidays. Her efforts proved fruitful as the growing number of Daughters branches caught the attention of the Sons. A New York Sons of Temperance Convention was planned for early 1852 in Albany and women were invited to send delegates. For the first time in history a significant number of women from all walks of life were engaged in public affairs.

As Anthony and a number of women were assigned seats at the convention it appeared that the great barrier to woman's participation in public life was being torn down. However, when Anthony rose to address a motion, the convention chairman silenced her. He forcefully explained that the women were invited to the convention not to be heard but to listen and to learn. Angry and indignant, Anthony, followed only by a few courageous women, walked out of the convention hall. Anthony and fellow delegate Lydia Mott organized a meeting for the next day at the Hudson Street Presbyterian Church. At the meeting Anthony's proposal for a Woman's State Temperance Convention won overwhelming approval and she was given the responsibility to organize it.

Anthony showcased her managerial and leadership abilities while putting together the April convention. With very little assistance, Susan B. Anthony wrote the necessary letters, reserved a hall, arranged for advertising and speakers and confirmed the attendance of some of the most prominent men and women in the state. Elizabeth Cady Stanton gladly accepted Anthony's invitation to speak while Horace Greeley promised to publish in his New York *Tribune* reports of the convention and devote as much space as possible to the speech texts.

The convention was a huge success and it generated a great enthusiasm among the 500 women in attendance. It received wide publicity in New York and to a lesser degree around the nation. Later in the convention the Woman's State Temperance Society was formed with Elizabeth Cady Stanton elected president and Amelia Bloomer and Susan B. Anthony as secretaries. Impressed with her efforts to insure the quality of this convention, the delegates gave Anthony responsibility for the bulk of the future work. She was appointed state agent with the power to solicit and collect donations, organize sister societies, issue membership certificates and perform all activities she deemed necessary to promote the Society and the purposes for which it was organized. It was Anthony's leadership, hard work and determination which made the convention a success.

By this time the Sons of Temperance had changed its name to the Men's State Temperance Society. They scheduled a state convention for June in Syracuse and again they invited the women to send delegates. Secretaries Bloomer and Anthony made the trip to Syracuse again hoping that the barriers working against them would finally be dissolved. As the convention opened, a great excitement filled the hall. Would the women present their credentials and effectively become part of the convention? Would the men and/or the significant number of clergy delegates permit them to do so?

After the opening formalities were concluded, delegate Dr. Mandeville rose to speak on the issue of the presence and participation of women. In a vulgar and extremely hostile oratory he denounced all women who actively took part in the temperance cause. He continued by saying that all such movements by women must be muzzled and torn out by the roots. He described women who participated in social issues such as this as a "hybrid species, half man and half woman, belonging to neither sex." The speech greatly polarized the audience as delegates on both sides of the issue yelled for recognition to speak. With the chair unable to restore order, the convention was utter pandemonium. Finally, after a hot June morning and afternoon of debate, a vote was taken and the women were not allowed to continue as delegates. Insulted and disappointed but determined as ever, Anthony and Bloomer left the hall to organize a meeting for that evening at a local church. Their event drew a full audience while scarcely 50 participants remained at the men's convention. Thrilled by this success, the women scheduled a convention for September in Syracuse.

Temperance, however was not to be the thrust of this convention; a wide variety of woman's rights issues were to be discussed at the three-day event. The most widely held belief however, was that women deserved the right to vote. Almost every speaker affirmed that only the ballot would emancipate women from their socially and politically impotent status. Lucretia Mott was elected president and again Susan B. Anthony was appointed secretary. Although the office of secretary does not carry the prestige granted the president, Anthony enjoyed and preferred her usual role as secretary. It not only gave her a voice in the organization's decision making process as a member of the executive board, but it offered an outlet for her skill as an organizer and administrator. Although she was extremely busy at the conventions, the majority of her work was done outside the convention halls—in the field going door to door on winter days asking men and women to sign petitions and donate money to the cause. These were the trenches in which the women fought the battle for their equality.

The convention was significant because of the large attendance—over 2000 women from eight states and Canada attended the affair. The real importance of the event was that it was the first major gathering of women to discuss these controversial issues. The Seneca Falls Convention of 1848 gained national attention but the poorly publicized event was not well attended. Since Seneca Falls, radical ideas such as women voting and owning property had only been discussed in private. By thrusting these ideas into public discourse, the Syracuse Woman's Rights Convention of 1852 was the spark that ignited the woman's rights movement. And Secretary Anthony's leadership was the fuel which kept the issues burning for the second-half of the nineteenth century.

The excitement and hope the convention had created was tempered however, by the public's reaction. Opponents of the movement often did not simply attack its merits or the reasoning behind the ideology; their criticisms all too frequently were personal smears and degradation of women in general. This excerpt from the New York *Herald* describing the convention not only exemplifies the insulting and often cruel nature of their opponents but also characterizes the prevailing nineteenth century American's mind-set:

> Who are these women? (W)hat do they want? What are the motives that impel them to this action? Some of them are old maids, whose personal charms were never very attractive and who have been sadly slighted by the masculine gender in general; some of them women who have been badly mated . . . mannish women , like hens that crow.
>
> How did woman first become subject to man as she is now all over the world? By her nature, her sex . . . therefore doomed to subjection; but happier than she would be in any other condition, just because it is the law of nature. The women themselves would not have this law reversed. It is a significant fact that even Mrs. Swisshelm, who formerly ran about to all such gatherings from her husband, is now "a keeper at home," and condemns these Conventions in her paper. How does this happen? Because after weary years of unfruitfulness, she has at length got her rights in the shape of a baby. This is the best cure for this mania, and we would recommend a trial of it to all who are afflicted.
>
> What do the leaders of the Woman's Rights Convention want? They want to vote . . to be members of Congress . . . They want to fill all other posts which men are ambitious to occupy—to be lawyers, doctors, captains of vessels, and generals in the field. How funny it would sound in the newspapers that Lucy Stone, pleading a cause, took suddenly ill in the pains of parturition, and perhaps gave birth to a bouncing baby boy in court! . . . A similar event might happen on the floor of Congress, in a storm at sea, or in the tempest of battle, and then what is to become of the woman legislator?

The Syracuse *Daily Star* took also condemned the convention:

> Perhaps we owe an apology for having given publicity to the mass
> of corruption, heresies, ridiculous nonsense, and reeking vulgarities
> which these bad women have vomited forth for the past three days. . .
>
> The convention adjourned *sine die* last evening at ten o'clock, and,
> for the credit of our city, we hope its members will adjourn out of town
> as soon as possible, and stay adjourned, unless they can come among us
> for more respectful business. Syracuse has become a by-word all
> through the country because of the influence which goes out from these
> foolish conventions held here, and it is high time that we be looking
> after our good name.

Reactions such as these were an indication to the women that the battle for social and political equality was just beginning.

The leadership of the Woman's State Temperance Society had allowed men to participate and become members but restricted them from becoming officers of the organization. But in early 1853 men and many of the women believed it wrong not to allow men to hold offices within the organization—that the women were restricting men in the same way women were being discriminated against. The women officers skeptically acquiesced and men soon dominated the organizational meetings, changed the name to the People's League and forced Elizabeth Cady Stanton from the presidency. Although the People's League folded within two years, the women had been removed from the temperance movement.

This frustrating experience taught the young Susan B. Anthony a great lesson: positive social change in the status of women could not be accomplished until women were political equals. In a journal entry she explained:

> . . . I was made to feel the great evil of woman's utter dependence
> on man for the necessary means to aid reform movements. I never
> before took in so fully the grand idea of pecuniary independence.
> Woman must have a purse of her own, and how can this be, so long as
> the law denies to the wife all right to both the individual and joint

earnings? There is no true freedom for woman without the possession
of equal property rights, and these can be obtained only through
legislation. If this be so the sooner the demand is made the sooner it
will be granted.

It was clear to Anthony that to have social status equal to that
of men, women would have to have the right to own property, (and
thus be able to be financially independent from their spouses) and
they would have to have the right to vote. This realization illustrates
how she was able to modify and update her vision to meet the needs
of the situation.

Anthony's job can also be described by the governmental net
analogy. Because the local, state and federal governments had
virtually neglected to include women under the protection of the
existing nets, Anthony had to construct the nets that would shield
women from social ills. She spent the remaining 50 years of her life
laboring to achieve those goals.

It is important to note the uniqueness of Anthony's
leadership-management style. Although women rarely had the
opportunity to learn or practice management and leadership skills,
she proved to be proficient at both. As secretary of the
organizations and conventions, she displayed a very efficient
management style. She accomplished the routine administrative
duties—letter writing, advertising, fund raising, support gathering,
event coordinating, etc.—with amazing speed, stamina and
competence. She was indeed, an efficient manager. As a member
of the executive boards, she was able to help shape the overall
organizational goals and determine the direction and tone of the
movement. In this way, she made the organizations and
conventions effective forces for social change.

The Civil War and Reconstruction

Until the outbreak of the Civil War, the woman's movement
had found a valuable ally in the abolitionist movement. Abolitionists
were one of the few groups that would grant women membership

and allow them to participate in their organizations. But the Civil War saw a decline in most reform movement activity as Americans were preoccupied with the conflict. Anthony realized that to preserve the progress made by her movement, she had to keep women active. If they were to cease activity, they might not regain their momentum after the War. With this in mind, Anthony and Cady Stanton organized a convention for "Loyal Women of the Nation" to meet and discuss a variety of war-related issues. Their call read in part:

> At this hour, the best word and work of every man and woman are imperatively demanded. To man, by common consent, is assigned the forum, the camp, and field. What is woman's legitimate work, and how best she may accomplish it, is worthy of our earnest counsel with one another . . . Woman is equally interested and responsible with man in the final settlement of this problem of self-government; therefore let none stand idle spectators now.

Women were kept active by many of the ideas discussed at this convention. These not only were an asset to the Northern side but it allowed them the opportunity to contribute, and in the minds of at least some, become partners with the men on the battlefield. By active participation in the War it was hoped that women could dismantle part of the argument that by their nature, their place was in the home. Early in the convention Anthony called the women to action:

> And now, women of the North, I ask you to rise up with earnest, honest purpose, and go forward in the way of right, fearlessly, as independent human beings, responsible to God alone for the discharge of every duty, for the faithful use of every gift, the good Father has given you. Forget conventionalisms; forget what the world will say, whether you are in your place or out of your place; think your best thoughts, speak your best words, do your best works, looking to your own conscience for approval.

Women were very active in the war effort. Hundreds of thousands of women were part of the Sanitary Commission with the charge of improving the soldier's field conditions. Activities included blanket and food distribution, inspecting the sanitary conditions of field hospitals and fund raising for relief efforts. A Brooklyn chapter raised over $300,000 in 1863 while the Chicago branch chipped in another $100,000 that year. Many women took their involvement a step further—at least 3000 Northern women staffed army hospitals as nurses despite low pay, terrible living and working conditions and frequent ridicule and animosity of the patients and doctors. In addition, as many as 400 northern women disguised themselves as men and became soldiers.

Although women played a significant and important role in the war effort, the woman's movement was still a great distance from its goal of suffrage. For at this same convention, the seeds of discontent between the abolitionists and the woman's rights activists were being sewn. There was debate on the merits of the resolution, "There never can be true peace in this Republic until the civil and political rights of all citizens of African descent and all women are practically established."

Sarah H. Halleck, among many, opposed the resolution, arguing:

> I would make the suggestion that those who approve of this resolution can afford to give way, and allow that part of it which is objectionable to be stricken out. The negroes have suffered more than the women, and the women, perhaps can afford to give them preference. Let it stand as regards to them, and blot out the word "woman." It may possibly be woman's place to suffer. At any rate, let her suffer, if, by that means, *man*kind may suffer less.

Susan B. Anthony rebutted her argument:

> This resolution . . . merely makes the assertion that in a true democracy, in a genuine republic, every citizen who lives under the government must have the right of representation. You remember the

maxim, "Governments derive their just powers from the consent of the governed." This is the fundamental principle of democracy; and before our Government can be a true democracy—before our republic can be placed upon lasting and enduring foundations—the civil and political rights of every citizen must be practically established. This is the assertion of the resolution. It is a philosophical statement. It is not because women suffer, it is not because slaves suffer, it is not because of any individual rights or wrongs—it is the simple assertion of the great fundamental truth of democracy that was proclaimed by our Revolutionary fathers. I hope the discussion will no longer be continued as the comparative rights or wrongs of one class over another. The question before us is: Is it possible that peace and union shall be established in this country; is it possible for this Government to be a true democracy, a genuine republic, while one-sixth or one-half of the people are disenfranchised?

Although the resolution was passed, Halleck's statement of opposition was an early form of the argument that would eventually exclude women from the social and political reforms of the Reconstruction period.

After the Civil War, the Thirteenth Amendment was passed which abolished slavery. Once slavery was eradicated the next logical step for the enfranchisement of blacks was granting them the rights of citizenship that were guaranteed in the proposed Fourteenth Amendment. While Congress was debating this issue in 1866 the exact wording of the Amendment set women and abolitionists at odds—the term "male" had been included as a requisite for citizenship.

Anthony declared in many of her speeches in support of the Civil War that the issue behind the conflict was freedom and that with a Northern victory all Americans would be free and equal as the Declaration of Independence maintained. But abolitionists were concerned that a fight to include women in the reforms would weaken the opportunity for blacks. They refused to aid and include women on the grounds that it was the "Negro's Hour." The Senate debate of 1866 focused on this question. Some, as Senator Johnson, were adamantly opposed to woman suffrage:

> Ladies have duties peculiar to themselves which cannot be discharged by anybody else; the nurture and education of their children, the demands upon them consequent upon the preservation of their household; and they are supposed to be more or less in their proper vocation when they are attending to those particular duties. But independent of that, I think if it were submitted to the ladies—I mean the ladies in the true acceptation of the term—of the United States, the privilege would not only not be asked for, but would be rejected. I do not think the ladies of the United States would agree to enter into a canvass, and to undergo what is often the degradation of seeking to vote . . . I rather think they would feel it, rather than a privilege, a dishonor.

Senator Frelinghuysen offered a similar argument:

> I confess a little surprise at the remark which has so frequently been made in the Senate, that there is no difference in granting suffrage to colored citizens and extending it to the women of America. The difference, to my mind, is as wide as the earth. As I understand it, we legislate for classes, and the women of America as a class do vote now . . . Do not the American people vote in this Senate to-day on this question? Do they not vote in the House of Representatives? So the women of America vote by their faithful and true representatives, their husbands, their brothers, their sons; and no true man will go to the polls and deposit his ballot without remembering that true and loving constituency that he has at home.

Others, such as Senator Buckalew, were opposed to woman suffrage on the grounds that enlarging the number of electors would increase political corruption:

> Will not these new electors you propose to introduce be more approachable than men who now vote to corrupt all influences? Will

they not be more passionate, and therefore more easily influenced by the demagogue? Will they not be more easily caught and enraptured by superficial declamation, because more incapable of profound reflection? Will not their weakness render them subservient to the strong and their ignorance to the artful?

It was not only opponents of the women that were omitting them from the reforms. Senator Wilson, a woman suffrage supporter, explained his rationale for the exclusion:

> . . . I will vote now or at any other time for woman suffrage, if . . . any . . . Senator will offer it as a distinct, separate measure, I am unalterably opposed to connecting that question with the pending question of negro suffrage. The question of negro suffrage is now an imperative necessity; a necessity that he should possess it for his own protection; a necessity that he should possess it that the nation may preserve its power, its strength, and its unity.

With the term "male" included, the Fourteenth Amendment became the law of the land in 1868. Susan B. Anthony and the woman's rights activists just wanted what was right. They did not want to oppose or compete with those advocating suffrage for blacks—they too argued the cause. Anthony did not want a debate on the comparative rights and wrongs subjected to the classes. She simply wanted the United States government to do what it promised in principle but it denied in practice. But, as was becoming an all too familiar occurrence, her cause was brushed aside and defeated by those in power.

The defeat not only split the woman and abolitionist movements, but it also divided the political support that the woman's movement had received in the past. When Horace Greeley opposed the inclusion of women in the Fourteenth Amendment, women lost a voice in the press and a substantial financial donor. The Republican party had championed the reform movements during the 1850s, but abandoned women on the Fourteenth Amendment. A further disappointment was that neither Democrats nor Republicans would endorse woman suffrage in their platform. The Civil War and Reconstruction period was a great opportunity for woman's rights progress, but as with so many other opportunities, their cause was defeated despite the best efforts of the women. Without a vision to guide her, these times of defeat and despair could have consumed her, but the vision of a better future for women provided the strength and motivation to begin anew.

The Kansas Campaign and the *Revolution*

In 1867 two amendments requiring a majority of the popular vote were proposed in Kansas. These amendments would have allowed women and blacks the right to vote in that state. This created a national excitement as it was the first time that such legislation had been put to a popular vote in the history of the United States. Activists in Kansas believed that a strong unified campaign could produce a victory for both measures. Because the defeat and split with the abolitionists had left the woman's groups broke, Anthony and Cady Stanton were forced to raise funds just to buy train tickets to get to Kansas. Finally, in late August they left New York to help organize and assist the Kansas campaign. They were scheduled to speak in towns all throughout Kansas everyday from September 2 through November 6. This grueling schedule was nothing new to Anthony as she had nearly frozen to death while conducting a petition drive in New York state during the terrible winter of 1854. The weather in Kansas would be better than her experience of 1854 but the living and traveling conditions would not.

Immediately upon their arrival in Kansas the two women set out on their speaking tour. Again they worked very well together— Cady Stanton was the headline speaker for the evening meetings while Anthony utilized her great skill as an organizer serving as the general manager. This gave her the responsibility to reserve and prepare a suitable hall, advertise the event, distribute and sell their literature and account for their finances. If she was not too exhausted after her long day of preparation, Anthony usually gave a short speech at the meeting. She did, however, have a great impact on the direction and tone of the campaign. She emphasized that the struggle in Kansas was part of the broader struggle for all women of the nation to obtain their social, economic and political equality.

The assemblies were great events in the frontier towns, but the primitive conditions of frontier life tempered their success. All travel in Kansas was done by wagon or stagecoach over the wind-swept, bumpy and rutted prairie. Rivers and streams were forded as bridges were still a rarity. The food they ate was a nutritionist's nightmare—usually the meat was canned or served submerged in grease. When vegetables were available they were frequently canned. The bread was soda-raised, the fruit was dried and the only available coffee additive was sorghum. After such a meal—washed down with alkaline water—the women began the nightly battle with bedbugs. A frontier fact of life, the pesky insects infested their hair, clothing and belongings. Anthony wrote many letters to family describing her and Cady Stanton's sleepless nights of discomfort and their efforts to rid themselves of the "tormentors."

Although the meetings were successful, the logistics of organizing meetings on such short notice became a near impossibility for Anthony. Eventually she parted with Cady Stanton and organized a campaign headquarters in Lawrence. From there she made advance arrangements for Cady Stanton and ex-Governor Charles Robinson, who proved to be a formidable ally in the campaign.

Politics played an important and deciding role in the Kansas Campaign of 1867. Republicans, backing the Negro-suffrage measure, initially voiced no support for the woman suffrage amendment. Further complicating the issue was a proposed liquor law which would have required all liquor agents to obtain signatures of half of the men and half of the women in the state before the government could grant them a liquor license. With their past ties to the temperance movement, the liquor lobby feared that women would support the proposed law. Women as a group never voiced an opinion on the liquor issue because they were focused solely on the issue of woman suffrage. However, the widely-publicized fears of the liquor lobby had done their damage—Republicans and many interest groups now openly voiced their opposition to suffrage for women.

In the November election both amendments failed. Out of approximately 30,000 votes, women received 9,070 while blacks garnered 10,843. The results were a bitter disappointment to the women as another opportunity was lost and their labors proved fruitless. With the effect of pouring salt on the women's open wounds, they were blamed by many for the failure of the Negro-suffrage initiative.

Although his surprise announcement of support failed to change the outcome of the election, the eccentric Democrat George Francis Train did provide much-needed financial backing toward the end of the campaign. Train was a wealthy businessman who championed liberal causes and dabbled in politics. Train was tall, slender and had dark curly hair. He wore flashy clothing including lavender gloves. People flocked to listen to—and see—the gifted orator express his often radical beliefs. Many believed that Train's support of women was a political ploy; he hoped that once women were given the ballot, they would support his presidential aspirations.

Motives aside, he did provide a boost for the cause. He offered Anthony the proprietorship of a weekly newspaper titled the *Revolution*. Elizabeth Cady Stanton and long-time woman's rights advocate Parker Pillsbury were made contributing editors. The periodical's motto was "men, their rights and nothing more, women, their rights and nothing less." It had been Anthony's ambition to have a paper devoted to her cause but the financial backing was never available. Train also offered Anthony and Cady Stanton a luxurious return trip to New York with numerous speaking engagements along the route to announce the new periodical. Anthony sold many $2 annual subscriptions to the *Revolution* on their much publicized journey home.

The excitement, however, was short-lived. Train retained limited space to express his views on current affairs, but his editorial content quickly became controversial as it was no more than propaganda for his political and financial schemes. Advertisers became leery of the paper and the *Revolution* soon experienced financial woes. To make matters worse, the whimsical Train, a staunch supporter of Ireland independence, left the country for Dublin where he was promptly arrested, tried and sentenced to life in prison. Although his sentence was commuted to deportation, he had lost interest in the *Revolution*. By 1871 the paper was defunct with a debt of $10,000. Another opportunity was lost and another dream was crushed but this disappointment failed to extinguish Anthony's burning determination. After 20 years of degradation, failure and frustration she was still devoted to her cause and ready to labor and fight for the realization of its goals.

The United States Vs. Susan B. Anthony

In her twenty year struggle for woman's equality, Anthony had pled her case to the people, she had tried to reason with the men who occupied the White House and she had appealed to various state and national legislative bodies all in vain. The one avenue she had not explored to achieve universal suffrage was the judicial system. Because the Fourteenth and Fifteenth Amendments, passed in 1868 and 1870, did not specifically deny women the right to vote, many people believed that it actually granted them suffrage. Anthony was determined to test this theory and vote using the following argument. The two Amendments say that "All persons born or naturalized in the United States . . . are citizens. No State shall make or enforce any law which shall abridge the privileges or immunities of citizens of the United States;" and "The right of citizens to vote shall not be denied." Therefore, all women, born or naturalized in the United States, should inherently have the right to vote.

Anthony's hometown paper urged citizens to register to vote because it was their civic duty in a democracy. Anthony persuaded 15 women to accompany her and register for the November 1872 election. The women were met with resistance by the election inspectors but Anthony recited her argument and, after much debate, they reluctantly registered the women. In all, Anthony induced 50 women to register for the election. Although she was now registered, Anthony expected that she would have to sue the election officials on election day to get to vote. To prepare for this she asked several attorneys to give opinions on her argument. None were even willing to hear her case until she talked with Henry R. Selden, a prominent member of the bar and former judge. He listened to Anthony, agreed with her arguments and took her case confident that it was a winnable one.

On November 5, 1872 Anthony cast her ballot with no resistance at the poll. News reports of the acceptance of the women's votes were widespread. Throughout the country stories and editorials filled the newspapers and surprisingly few of the comments describing the event were hostile to the women in describing the event. Two weeks later, however, Anthony was arrested by Deputy United States Marshal E. J. Kenney. Her bail was set at $500; however, she refused to pay and applied for a *writ of habeus corpus.* The *writ* was not only denied by United States District-Judge H. K. Hall, but he increased her bail to $1,000 as well. She was arrested and indicted because she "did knowingly, wrongfully and unlawfully vote." Unfamiliar with legal forms, Anthony allowed Selden to pay her $1000 bond. Although her attorney knew this action would not permit Anthony an appeal to the Supreme Court, he said that he could not see a lady he respected put in jail.

In the interim between her arrest and trial, Anthony traveled to Illinois and Ohio to speak at the state suffrage conventions. She traveled throughout the Midwest lecturing in many cities and towns and on her return trip to New York, she presided over the National Woman Suffrage Convention in Washington D.C. She seized every opportunity to describe the injustice of the case against her, and to explain the merits of her Constitutional argument allowing all women the right to vote. Her appeals gained attention throughout the national press while both her supporters and opponents anxiously awaited her day in court.

She also spoke throughout Albany County, New York explaining how the Constitution gave women the right to vote. The U.S. district attorney threatened to move the trial to a new location on the grounds that her efforts were making the assembly of an impartial jury impossible. Anthony retorted that wherever the trial was moved she and other women would make similar efforts to inform citizens of woman's Constitutional right to vote. She added that her efforts could not be a crime since she was merely reading the Constitution. The trial was moved to the U.S. Circuit Court in Canandaigua, New York and scheduled for June 17, 1873.

The trial opened that afternoon with Assistant-Justice Ward Hunt presiding. Former President Millard Fillmore and many prominent members of New York society filled the gallery. After Selden and his counterpart, United States District Attorney Richard Crowley, made their opening remarks, Selden testified that he advised Anthony to vote because he believed women possessed that Constitutional right. Selden then called Anthony to the stand, but Judge Hunt prohibited her from testifying on the grounds that, because she was a woman, she was not a competent witness.

After the closing arguments, Judge Hunt *directed* the jury to return with a guilty verdict. Anthony's legal counsel was outraged and adamantly objected to the action because a judge does not have that power, but Hunt overruled Selden. Hunt read from his written statement pronouncing Anthony guilty of unlawful voting. Many of those involved in the case believed that Hunt had prepared the statement prior to the trial. After he refused Selden's motion that the jury at least be polled, Judge Hunt dismissed the jury—none having said a word throughout the trial. Many jurors admitted after the trial that they would have voted Anthony "not guilty."

On the following day, Selden cited seven legal reasons in arguing for a new trial, but Hunt again refused his motion. Hunt then asked Anthony if she had anything to say before he sentenced her. Anthony stood and said:

Yes, your honor, I have many things to say; for in your ordered verdict of guilty you have trampled under foot every vital principle of

our government. My natural rights, my civil rights, my political
rights, my judicial rights, are all alike ignored. Robbed of my
fundamental privilege of citizenship, I am degraded from the status of a
citizen to that of a subject; and not only myself individually but all of
my sex are, by your honor's verdict, doomed to political subjection
under this so-called republican form of government.

During her attempt to explain the injustices of her trial, Hunt
interrupted Anthony six times insisting that the court could not allow
her to regurgitate the trial. Anthony, deprived of her rights to vote
and to a fair trial, was sentenced to pay a fine of $100 and the costs
of prosecution. In a response that revealed some of the despair she
had endured for twenty years, Anthony told the court:

May it please your honor, I will never pay a dollar of your unjust
penalty. All the stock in trade I possess is a debt of $10,000, incurred
by publishing my paper—The *Revolution*—the sole object of which
was to educate all women to do precisely as I have done, rebel against
your man-made unjust, unconstitutional forms of law, which tax, fine
and imprison women, while denying them the right of representation
in the government; and I will work on with might and main to pay
every dollar of that honest debt, but not a penny shall go to this unjust
claim. And I shall earnestly and persistently continue to urge all
women to the practical recognition of the old Revolutionary maxim,
"Resistance to tyranny is obedience to God."

Anthony never did pay the fine. Throughout the nation there
was considerable support for Anthony. Even opponents of woman
suffrage were quick to castigate Hunt for his flagrant snubbing of
Anthony's Constitutional right to a fair trial by jury. Another
opportunity for women was dashed, and, with her right to appeal
snuffed, it was painfully clear to Anthony that for women to obtain
the ballot the states would have to pass appropriate legislation. With
sufficient state support an Amendment to the Constitution could then
be introduced with a good chance of ratification. Anthony began
work on what would eventually be known as the Susan B. Anthony

Amendment (the Nineteenth Amendment) which enfranchised women into the American form of government and finally made the United States a true representative democracy.

Explaining Her Success

Although a Constitutional Amendment giving women the right to vote was not ratified until 1920, 14 years after her death, no one person can be praised more than Susan B. Anthony for the accomplishment. Anthony, Elizabeth Cady Stanton and Lucretia Mott were the "Founding Mothers" of the women's movement. They had three great challenges: first, they had to make the nation aware that a great inequality existed in the American form of government; second, they had to dismantle the nineteenth century mind-set that women were inherently inferior to men; and finally, they had to persuade the establishment to act upon the inequality. Thus, her success cannot be measured in terms of programmatic or legislative change alone. Discussion of Anthony's success should also include how she changed the attitude and belief structure of her era.

Early in her career as a woman's rights activist, her opponents rarely gave statements that were rationally debatable. Frequently the opposition was focused on the women themselves in the form of a personal insult. Often they merely cited "Biblical evidence" that women were by nature inferior and that their place was in the home. Some opponents were polite—such as the man who, upon listening to Anthony speak in 1853 said, "Miss Anthony, that was a magnificent address. But I must tell you that I would rather see my wife or daughter in her coffin that hear her speaking as you did before a public assembly." Some opponents were hostile—such as when she was yelled down at the 1852 temperance convention at which she was called a member of a "hybrid species, half man and half woman, belonging to neither sex."

By the 1870s public support for woman suffrage was more widespread and the arguments used against Anthony were less personal and more philosophical in nature. Although arguments such as "women don't want to vote" and "women already vote through the men in their lives" were still insulting and equally frustrating, they were at least statements that could be debated.

At the turn of the century support for woman suffrage was still growing and a common belief concerning the movement was that "I suppose it is bound to happen sooner or later." It is easy to speculate from our vantage point in the last decade of the twentieth century that woman suffrage was inevitable. Without Susan B. Anthony pulling, pushing and prodding a sluggish establishment to pass legislation while she molded and shaped societal norms for 50 years of her life, the Nineteenth Amendment might have been passed as the Twenty-fifth Amendment. Susan B. Anthony, the saleswoman of the woman's movement, proved through hard work, determination, persistence and a resilient character that, indeed, failure is impossible.

THE WAY SHE DID BUSINESS

Anthony's success was not only due to her vision and resilient character. The methodology she used to secure change earned her enormous credibility which made much of the progress possible. She disliked the limelight and did not seek attention for herself—only for the cause. She saw her efforts as the means to an end, not the end itself. This unselfishness gave her work an altruistic flavor and compelled people to give her support. Without a cooperative attitude and high ethical standards, all of Susan B. Anthony's determination would have produced far fewer results.

Cooperation Vs. Competition

Competition is inherent to a capitalistic society such as ours. Good healthy competition forces each of us to perform to the best of our abilities. The freedom of competition in the United States has elevated a small, fragile and weak confederation of colonies to a social, military, economic and political superpower. While competition brings out the best in humans, it can also bring out the worst—corruption, fraud and greed. To an organization or a movement, there is an important difference between internal and external competition.

Competition within an organization can be dangerous. Left alone without supervision and control, it can hinder its efforts or even destroy the organization itself. The Reagan administration exemplified this at the end of his second term as president. The internal competition between aides, cabinet members and advisors grew out of control resulting in public argument and scandal. Resultantly, the administration accomplished very little during that time. As individuals and factions fought for control, the group's efforts were focused away from executing Reagan's programs and toward petty bickering, back-stabbing and attempts to "get ahead" and to "get even." The resulting "kiss and tell" books written by staff members and even the president's wife drew attention away from productivity and threw the government into chaos.

However, internal competition can be healthy in certain situations. Contests in fund-raising, charity drives and other instances where all involved benefit rather than only the victor, can provide additional external motivation to realize the vision. They must be carefully monitored and controlled to produce the desired result.

Competition external to an organization also can be dangerous. Poor judgment in a competitive atmosphere can be fatal to an organization—a lesson learned from the Watergate break-in and scandal. This type of competition can be beneficial, for example, between Coke and Pepsi; General Motors, Ford and Chrysler; and AT&T, U.S. Sprint and MCI, as their efforts to "better" the others can benefit the organizations and to all those served by them. External competition can be a great motivator and a boost for morale, but it must also be monitored and controlled. Internal and external competition can both be beneficial and detrimental; the determining factor is usually the presence or absence of good judgement and high ethical standards.

Susan B. Anthony and Elizabeth Cady Stanton were both well aware of the competitive forces present in the woman's movement and in their relationship. A credit to their wisdom is their realization that cooperation can often be a more powerful and more effective force than competition. Their ability to work together kept the movement focused on its purpose and allowed each to utilize her individual strengths while compensating for the other's weaknesses.

Their relationship is a perfect model of win/win strategy. They understood that a victory for one was a victory for the cause, which was of the utmost importance. Both realized that victory and success were not zero-sum games—that a victory for one did not mean a defeat for the other. By working together they were able to maximize each others wins, and thus, achieve more for their cause. By utilizing this win/win strategy, the resulting products were much greater than the sum of their individual efforts.

Understanding the role of each in the woman's movement is necessary to better understand their cooperative working relationship. Cady Stanton was frequently elected president of the organizations and conventions while Anthony was appointed secretary. Because she had seven children to raise, Cady Stanton rarely ventured from her Seneca Falls home for extended periods. This allowed her to attend the many, but short, annual and semi-annual meetings. She spent her remaining time child-rearing and writing on woman's rights issues. Cady Stanton was a prolific and gifted writer and speaker, which made her a highly visible and highly regarded member of the movement. Virtually everything she wrote, did and said was reported by the newspapers which afforded her a celebrity-like status.

Anthony, without family commitments, was perpetually busy with her secretarial duties. Because she was busy with the cause everyday, Anthony was a more active and guiding force than Cady Stanton, but because her numerous administrative efforts were never reported in the newspapers, she was less visible than her colleague. Anthony excelled at the necessary but thankless responsibilities of secretary. On only a few occasions, including the Kansas campaign, did Cady Stanton possess the time and desire to get her hands dirty in the trenches with Anthony and partake in the field-work. Perhaps because of this Cady Stanton was perceived by most as the movement's stateswoman—a role she performed exceptionally well, and one vital to the success of the movement. The important factor in their relationship, and the resulting success of the cause, was their awareness and acceptance of their respective roles. Both Cady Stanton and Anthony knew their individual strengths and weaknesses and performed the tasks each was capable of, while allowing the other to do the same. Infighting would have only split the movement and focused the nation's attention away from woman's rights issues.

Contemporary psychologists might explain the success of this exceptional working relationship by the diverseness of their personalities. Cady Stanton can be described as a "type B" personality: easy-going, emotional and externally motivated. Anthony was a strong "type A," exhibiting serious task-oriented, self-motivated behavior. As communicators, they complemented each other to produce some of the best political writing and oratory of their time. Both possessed a great ethos on the stage and behind the pen, but Cady Stanton's strength was in the emotional appeal of the words—pathos. Conversely, Anthony was analytical, developing logical Aristotelian arguments—she had a gift for logos. Both able communicators by themselves, together they raised oratory and the written word to a much higher level—one not thought possible of women of that time. Anthony often visited Cady Stanton in Seneca Falls where they collaborated on many speeches, letters and strategies for the woman's rights cause. In 1863 the women wrote a brilliant letter to President Lincoln applauding his emancipation of the slaves and urging executive action for the equality of women.

They shared a strong friendship and a great mutual respect which grew stronger over the decades they worked together. Throughout their entire relationship, both personal and professional, they operated as equals. The fact that Cady Stanton was frequently elected president of the many organizations and conventions only pleased Anthony. She felt no envy or held any malice toward her friend as she accepted the position of secretary. Anthony realized that their cooperative relationship was best for the movement, when she could organize and toil out of the lime light while Cady Stanton promoted the movement as a jovial stateswoman. Often this would result in newspapers reacting favorably to Cady Stanton and critically of Anthony, but that was of no consequence as long as the cause moved forward.

Ethics

Susan B. Anthony's high ethical standards of conduct throughout her 50 year involvement in the woman's movement was a contributing factor to her success. By putting sound ethical judgement into practice, Anthony kept the nation's attention focused on legal and political progress for women. Without her leadership in this area, the nation could have become preoccupied with stories of fraud, fund mismanagement, sex scandals and infighting among the movement's membership—any or all of which would have been detrimental to the cause.

In her role as secretary, Anthony was responsible for the accounting of funds donated to the movement through its various members and organizations. Virtually all donations were in the form of cash and, thus, untraceable. After departing her comfortable life as a teacher in Canajoharie, Anthony never held a formal job or gained income outside of the movement. She did use a small portion of the funds donated to live and travel as she canvassed the country on her numerous speaking tours and petition drives. Despite the great and obvious opportunity to upgrade her modest lifestyle, Anthony never took advantage of her position. Never did she use donations or movement funds for personal gain or contrary to their purpose of advancing the woman's movement. Often she would have to tap her personal savings account to pay for the printing of pamphlets, brochures and speeches she distributed with her lectures. She replenished her personal account only through the admission receipts to her lectures. Excess receipts and other donations she used for printing, promotion and speakers' honoraria and travel.

She might have used donations to repay the $10,000 debt owed from the failed *Revolution*. Sadly, Anthony was the only person involved with the newspaper—which included Cady Stanton, George Francis Train and suffragist Parker Pillsbury, among others—who felt obligated to repay the debt. It took Anthony six long years on the lecture circuit to reimburse the huge debt. Newspapers celebrated the announcement of her final payment with praise for Anthony. The Buffalo *Express* said, "Not one man in a thousand but who would have 'squealed,' 'laid down,' and settled at ten or twenty cents on the dollar." The Rochester *Post-Express* continued the praise, "There are a great many men who would have hidden behind their wives' pettycoats for a much smaller sum than $10,000 . . . Yet here is an example, in a woman, who our laws say is not fit to exercise the active and defensive principle of citizenship, that puts to shame the lives of nine hundred and ninety-nine in every thousand men."

Another example of Anthony's integrity benefitting the woman's movement occurred in 1872 amid a sex scandal involving three prominent supporters of the cause. In the 1860s, Henry Ward Beecher and Elizabeth Tilton had an affair. Soon thereafter, Elizabeth had confessed the relationship to her husband, Theodore, the publisher and New York businessman who was an ardent supporter and active in the cause. Beecher, a longtime friend of the Tiltons and supporter of the woman's movement, was the Pastor of the Plymouth Church in Brooklyn, New York and one of the most famous clergyman in America at the time. Anthony, a working colleague of all three, also considered each a personal friend. One evening as Anthony was arriving at the Tilton residence, Theodore threatened Elizabeth and left for the night. Scared and sobbing, Elizabeth proceeded to tell Anthony the details of the affair. Because of the ramifications that news of the affair could have on the movement, Anthony later informed Cady Stanton of the situation. Rumors of the event were almost common knowledge among the ranking members of the movement, as Elizabeth Tilton had confided in others after her talk with Anthony.

Cady Stanton made the mistake of relating the details to Victoria Woodhull. Woodhull was a young, outspoken radical feminist and president of the American branch of Karl Marx's International Workingman's Association. Woodhull and her sister, Tennie C. Claflin established the first female brokerage firm on Wall Street and operated a newspaper—*Woodhull and Claflin Weekly*. Suffragists were hesitantly supportive of Woodhull's involvement in the movement because she had been accused by Beecher of advocating "free love"—promiscuity. Woodhull brought energy, excitement, ability and wealth to the cause and many welcomed her support—commitment was the one trait she did not possess. Woodhull quickly climbed to the top of the National Woman Suffrage Association and fought for its control. In 1872 she sought its support for her nomination for president of the United States in her newly formed Equal Rights Party. Correctly sensing disaster, Anthony was able to prevent Woodhull from executing her plans. If Woodhull had succeeded, women would have lost the support of both Republicans and Democrats because neither would support a third political party. Woodhull's presidential aspirations not only were unsuccessful, but they put her in virtual financial ruin.

Having lost almost everything, Woodhull sought to retaliate against Beecher and the suffragists. In a lengthy story, she vindictively printed the explicit details of the Beecher-Tilton affair in one of the final issues of her paper. This created a national sensation similar to the Gary Hart-Donna Rice scandal of the late 1980s. Many close to the situation were eager to relate their account of the affair and grab a share of the limelight. Even Cady Stanton recited her version of the event and wrote editorials denouncing the clergyman Beecher as a hypocrite. Anthony was noticeably silent on the issue though reporters followed her every move hoping to overhear a juicy tidbit. She was offered huge sums of money for her story as she was Elizabeth Tilton's first confidante. Anthony was traveling and preparing for her trial for unlawful voting and refused to become a participant in what was becoming a media circus.

Had Anthony sold her story she could have earned thousands of dollars—all of which she could have used to repay the *Revolution* debt. But Anthony was wise and had integrity. Ending her silence on the situation would have only focused attention away from the suffrage movement and the realization of her vision. She also would have lost credibility in the eyes of many for selling out and spending her time on such a trivial issue. She could have used the event to grab her share of the limelight but that was not important to her. She had been and would always be devoted to the legal and political enfranchisement of women into American society. Lowering herself into insignificant matters would only have complicated her job and wasted time that she could have spent working toward her vision.

Her silence and indifference to the issue won her the admiration of even her opponents. Despite their disappointment in not hearing her story, newspapers praised her integrity to take the moral high-ground during the scandal. To Anthony, tarnishing the reputations of members only tarnished the movement itself. Soon the excitement of the Beecher-Tilton scandal subsided and suffragists continued their work.

*   *   *

America must confront many serious, complex and diverse problems as we prepare to enter the twenty-first century. Although Anthony taught her lessons of leadership in the nineteenth century, they still are of great value today. She was unique—a visionary with integrity and a win/win attitude, but resiliency was her trademark. Although John Kennedy spoke the words 55 years after she died, Anthony would have applauded the concept of his inaugural address—"All this will not be finished in the first hundred days. Nor will it be finished in the first thousand days, nor in the lifetime of this administration, nor even perhaps in our lifetime on this planet. But let us begin." Bearing in mind Kennedy's urgency and sense of duty and the successfulness of Anthony's determination, we must focus attention on our present crisis and prove again that failure is impossible.

Chapter 2

Harry S. Truman

Harry S. Truman rarely if ever suffered from his lack of a formal education. Although he is the most recent president not to receive a college degree, in terms of the leadership he provided the country, he was one of the best presidents of the United States. The story of Truman's life confirms that hard work, determination and a model moral character greatly contribute to living a successful life. He never had much money, but the accomplishments of his political career continue to enrich the lives of millions of Americans far beyond that possible from any material wealth. His ascent to the White House from humble beginnings is proof that no destiny is beyond reach. If, like Truman, we use leadership to make the most of our own opportunities, each of us can improve the quality of our life and the quality of American society.

Harry, the eldest of three Truman children, was born in Lamar, Missouri on May 8, 1884. In 1890 John Truman moved his family to a farm near Independence, Missouri where Harry grew up and, except for a stay in Washington D.C., resided for the rest of his life. It was the Missouri rural life that taught him the moral character of hard work, honesty and common sense that would make his career as a public official blossom.

Poor eyesight was one of the most important factors shaping the character and destiny of Harry S. Truman. At the age of five he was given glasses and his world focused into perspective. They did, however, isolate him from other boys of his age. Because he feared participation in sports would break his glasses, Harry found another activity appealing—he began reading. His interest lay primarily in histories and biographies. Mr. Truman once recounted that by the age of 14 he had read all of the 3000 books in the Independence library, which figures to be roughly a book a day for nine years. Although it is doubtful he read that much, it is safe to say he was an avid reader. The knowledge of the people and places he read about was important throughout his career. The vast knowledge he obtained through reading of Ancient Greece and Rome, the Middle and Far East, European history and the presidency of the United States, taught him how past people and events relate to present situations. As a result, Truman believed that all decisions must be based on an understanding of both past and present situations.

Reading was not the only force shaping the young Truman. The strong-willed Martha Ellen Truman had a profound influence on her son, Harry. She graduated from the Baptist Female College in Lexington, Missouri with a degree in music and art. In addition to his normal chores around the farm, Harry helped his mother in the kitchen and he took care of his baby sister. It was during this time, when the other boys were playing ball, that Mamma Truman bestowed upon her son a strong moral fiber. At the turn of the century, a boy who spent a lot of time with his mother rather than playing with the other boys often was labeled a "mamma's boy." This was not true in Harry's case. Anyone familiar with the strong will and wisdom of Martha Ellen Truman simply laughed at the idea of Harry being a momma's boy. In fact, Harry's childhood was anything but dull—he enjoyed both the giving and receiving of practical jokes.

In his late childhood, Harry and some friends met a few girls on the bank of the Missouri River for a picnic. Two of the boys put a message in a bottle and tossed it in the river to see if they would get a response. Truman and a few fellow pranksters invented two Mississippi Belles who wrote love letters back to the two gentlemen. Truman and his accomplices would send romantic letters and pictures to friends in Mississippi who were able to re-mail them with the proper postmark.   The victims believed the phony correspondence and soon the two were lovesick. Finally, the charade was exposed much to the despair and dismay of the two duped victims.

Harry worked at a drug store while in high school and after graduation he worked as a time keeper for the railroad. A few months later he went to work for a bank. Upon the death of his father, he quit the bank to work the family farm. Farming wasn't easy but it taught him that hard work was what it took to succeed in life. He worked the 160 acres until the United States entered World War I. Truman had been a First Lieutenant in the Army reserves, and after he was called up to active duty he was placed in command of Battery D of the 129th Field Artillery.

This was no easy task as the enlisted men of Battery D had a reputation of being a bunch of undisciplined, brawling Irishmen from Kansas City. They had already rid themselves of three commanding officers, and when they saw Lt. Truman, they assumed it wouldn't be long before the fourth was gone. Tom Murphy, a veteran of Battery D, explained that it was the Lieutenant's leadership the endeared the men to him:

> After the armistice he (Truman) had a furlough to go to Paris . . . and while he was gone, some of the men found some bottles of green cognac and we all got very drunk and disorderly. When Harry first came back, he didn't say a word, and I had . . . well, I had started over sleeping and missing reveille, and he called me in. I was a sergeant, and he called me in and said, "Sergeant, that business with the cognac was pretty disgusting, and I'm going to bust you!"
>
> I said, "Well, sir. I certainly do deserve it." He looked at me in the eye and paused for a minute, and then he said, "Okay. You go back and behave yourself now."
>
> I'm sure if I'd pleaded to keep my rank, he'd have busted me. But he appreciated the fact that I didn't do it, and after that . . . I'd . . . like most of the rest of Battery D, would do whatever we possibly could for Harry Truman.

After the War, he returned to Independence to marry his fiance; on June 28, 1919, Harry S. Truman married Elizabeth (Bess) Virginia Wallace. They had one daughter, Margaret, who wrote, among many very successful novels, a biography of her father. In 1922, after a brief business venture failed, Mr. Truman was elected Judge of Jackson County, Missouri. In this role as a county commissioner, he established himself as an honest politician independent of the powerful political machines. He was a friend of Tom Pendergast, the "boss" of Jackson County, who was thought by many to be corrupt. However, Mr. Truman was able to proudly affirm that Mr. Pendergast never asked him to perform a dishonest deed.

Truman was eventually elected presiding judge—the highest-ranking county official. In his two terms, he built the finest system of roads in the state. In 1934 and 1940, he was elected to the United States Senate. The special committee he established in 1941 to investigate the national defense program gained him national recognition. Although this was not his goal, it catapulted the unknown senator from Missouri into Franklin Roosevelt's choice for running mate in the 1944 presidential election. Truman was adamantly opposed to joining the ticket, but Roosevelt expressed to him that his refusal would split the Democratic party. Mr. Truman held the vice presidential post for a mere 84 days.

Truman's Presidency was one crisis after another. With each critical situation in the post-WWII era, Truman's policies became increasingly controversial. Pollsters gave him no chance to win reelection in 1948, but, in one of the biggest upsets in political history, Truman defeated Thomas Dewey. His second term was again plagued with intricate situations and difficult decisions but President Truman exhibited the leadership that likely prevented World War III.

Upon his retirement in 1953, he returned to Independence and built the Truman Library to house his presidential papers. Dedicated in 1957, it serves as a museum of his presidency and a research facility for scholars. One of his favorite activities in retirement was speaking to college students.

> . . . I have found myself becoming a kind of roving teacher. This is a role that has given me a great deal of happiness and satisfaction.

To me there is nothing more rewarding than to stand before young people and find them so vitally interested in everything pertaining to the affairs of the country and the world. I do not share the concern of some critics that our young people lack the quality and character of former generations. . . What impresses me more than anything else in the questions they ask me is in the range and variety of the interests of the young people. I find myself . . . as invigorated and as alert as I used to feel after a White House press conference.

The following is an examination of the wealth of leadership Mr. Truman displayed in three significant periods in his political career. These should be viewed as further lectures to the "young people" by the "roving teacher."

THE TRUMAN COMMITTEE

During Truman's bitter Senate campaign of 1940, he received hundreds of letters describing the gross mismanagement of government funds in the building of Fort Leonard Wood in Missouri. From his earlier work in the Military Subcommittee of the Senate Appropriations Committee, Truman was aware that favoritism in awarding government contracts and misuse of funds was characteristic of the military.

Senator Harry Truman was not a person who could watch this problem continue. Truman embarked on a 25,000 mile trek (which he paid for himself) from Florida to Michigan touring many of the defense installations. This one-month journey exposed to the Senator the need for a watchdog on the expanding defense program. In a speech to the Senate on February 10, 1941, Truman detailed the waste and corruption he had witnessed during his inspections.

His vision was to save money and lives by shaping the defense program to run efficiently and effectively respond to the mounting world tensions. Truman's objectives were not to restrict or cripple the defense program, because in 1940 he campaigned for a strong defense program. Rather, he wanted to make sure that the money was being spent wisely. Because he had an ideal and unique image of the future for the defense program, Truman and the committee members were able have a positive impact on the war effort.

Truman asked the Senate for its support of a resolution which would create a committee to investigate the Defense Program. On March 1, 1941 the Senate established the Senate Special Committee to Investigate the National Defense Program. As is tradition in Congress, the sponsor of the resolution is given the chairmanship of the new committee and thus, the "Truman Committee" was born.

It is interesting why support was given immediately to Truman's concerns. Representative Eugene Cox of Georgia had been making similar statements in the House. Cox was an anti-Roosevelt Democrat and his threat to the mounting war effort concerned the president. So when Senator Harry Truman, a loyal Roosevelt New-Dealer, voiced his outrage of the waste he had observed on his personal inspection tour, the administration was quick to give support to his ideas and, unbeknownst to Truman, erase Cox from the picture.

The Truman Committee investigated the national defense program from 1941 to 1948. Truman was the Chairman from its inception to August of 1944 when Roosevelt chose him to run on his ticket as vice president. The Committee's success was due largely to Truman's sense of foresight. His ability to think ahead and understand the consequences of his actions gave the Committee credibility, which, in turn, gave members the courage necessary to confront, question and expose problems in business, government and the military.

Foresight Results in Credibility

Truman's concern for the war effort was genuine. Prior to forming the Committee, the senator visited the Library of Congress to learn about a similar committee established in the early 1860s. As testimony to Truman's true desires for his committee, he read each volume of the transcripts and reports. The collection was of such length that it occupied a five foot shelf, but it yielded the senator much information. The Committee on the Conduct of the Civil War, however, was designed to be a thorn in the side of President Lincoln by Congressmen opposed to the conflict. Truman was resolved to not let history repeat itself. This information gave the senator and his efforts a large dose of credibility.

Two seeds had been planted in the senator's mind concerning the need for such an investigation. First, Harry Truman remembered the mismanagement affecting the defense program during World War I. All of the 116 probes had been conducted *after* the War. The findings of the investigations not only shocked the Congress but angered the American public. By 1920, there was nothing that could be done because the investigations were too late. In contrast to conducting a *post mortem*, Truman believed that one thorough investigation *before and during* the war would prevent waste and possibly save the lives of American servicemen. He was correct.

A second seed was planted in his days as the presiding judge of Jackson County, Missouri. Truman's devotion to a modern county road project faced opposition from the public only because the officials preceding him had padded their own pockets (and those of the contractors) with the money that was earmarked for the roads. Truman saw the need for a watchdog of public funds. With a relatively low budget (compared to the national defense budget) this could be and was accomplished by one man—Harry Truman. But with a defense budget in the billions of dollars, Truman would need help.

The seven original Committee members were a young group—five were serving their first terms in the Senate. Including Truman, they were Tom Connally, Texas Democrat; Carl Hatch, New Mexico Democrat; James Mead, New York Democrat; Mon Wallgren, Washington Democrat; Ralph Owen Brewster, Maine Republican; and Joseph Ball, Minnesota Republican. Because they believed the real power in Congress to be in the standing committees, senior Senators usually declined to serve on ad-hoc committees.   With a young membership came a desire from each member to make an impact in the Senate.   This committee assignment was a much better opportunity to receive recognition than through the hierarchies of their standing committees.   Truman included all the members in the work which kept them informed and interested.   With all seven members playing active parts in the investigations, not only did each feel the Committee's efforts were worthy of his time, but it also made it exceptionally efficient for a Congressional committee.

In addition to reading the reports of the Civil War Committee, Truman's sense of foresight led him to take four further steps to ensure that his Committee would indeed be functional: he did not design it to gain publicity; he insured that it would let the facts speak for themselves; he allowed and desired all members to share in the limelight; and Truman incorporated the assistance of non-member senators into the process.

First, the Committee did not seek headlines. Truman later explained that many of the findings could have been played up in the media but his goal was to save money and lives—not wallow in publicity. This thorough and professional approach to the investigation prevented pandemonium in the press and the public. Rather than creating a circus-like atmosphere with Truman the ringmaster feeding tales of corruption and waste to a frothing public, he took a calm, methodical and rational approach to the situation. Because he was careful not to disclose claims until they were substantiated and the investigations were complete, his Committee was viewed as credible and as an asset to the effort to win the war. This kept the focus of the American public off of the Committee and aimed it where it needed to be: arming America and the allies to defeat the Japanese and Germans.

Second, the Committee aimed its concerns at the conditions of the situation, not the people involved. The Committee never pointed blame at individuals, rather it simply allowed the facts to speak for themselves.   The findings may have been very embarrassing to some participants, but the reports never made recommendations on the removal of personnel. The Committee only made recommendations on the necessary steps that should be taken to rectify a situation. As a result of the Truman Committee investigations, many people did lose their jobs and go to jail, and many businesses lost their contracts. But the Committee only exposed the facts; further action, the Committee believed, was the responsibility of the appropriate agency—the military and/or the Department of Justice. This insulation from the punishment distribution prevented the Truman Committee from conducting witch-hunts and bestowed credibility upon it.

An example of the Truman Committee's desire to aim their concern at solving the exposed problems rather than at laying blame, is evident in the Committee's investigation of the Wright Aeronautical Corporation's Lockland, Ohio plant. The contract specified that Wright Aeronautical Corporation (WAC) would supply aircraft engines to the Government on a fixed-price basis. For this reason it was in the best interests of WAC to produce engines as quickly as possible. Because WAC had a reputation of building the finest aircraft and engines, it was granted an 'A' inspection rating by the Army Air Forces. This placed the prime responsibility for product inspection on WAC.

Soon thereafter, reports of flawed engines produced in the Lockland plant reached the Truman Committee. In the ensuing investigation, it was learned that many of the engines that had been approved for shipment were leaking gasoline. In addition, more than 25 percent of the engines built consistently failed during a three-hour test run.

The investigation discovered that the faulty engines were a result of poor inspection practices. "Army inspectors were refused access to precision instruments with which they might check suspected material. Their inspection was restricted to purely visual examination." The Committee's report stated that inspectors were coerced into approving defective products. It exposed cases where the company pressured its inspectors to pass defective material. Others were reprimanded for notifying army inspectors of flawed products. The committee also discovered that army inspectors were subjected to similar pressures and that one was actually transferred for rejecting "an engine that was leaking gasoline."

The approval of these defective engines and spare parts resulted in many tragic American service personnel deaths. Consequently, a number of Army Air Force and WAC personnel found themselves in jail. But the punishment was not the recommendation of the Truman Committee:

> The committee believes that misconduct of this character should be investigated promptly and that appropriate disciplinary action should follow immediately. . . the complete files of the committee on this matter have now been referred to the War Frauds Division (of the Department of Justice) for such action as deemed necessary.

Although it is difficult to ascertain an exact dollar figure, the Committee's investigation of Wright Aeronautical Corporation's Lockland plant saved the government hundreds of thousands of dollars in defective products. Its efforts also saved the lives of hundreds of aircraft pilots and crews.

The third step Truman took to ensure that his Committee would be functional and run smoothly was to let others share in the limelight. Truman perceived his duty as chairman to organize the Committee and develop the framework and boundaries of the investigations so they would be in harmony with his vision. Truman did not see himself as an indispensable member or the one fully responsible for its accomplishments. Committee members other than Truman read 17 of the 32 reports given to the Senate during Truman's four-year tenure as chairman. This resulted in members receiving attention and recognition exceeding any that Truman personally could have given them.

Fourth, Truman frequently allowed non-member senators to ask questions at hearings and become somewhat involved in the committee's work. Truman was very careful, however, not to allow non-members to grandstand. Their integration into the process was an important factor in the Committee gaining broad Senatorial support. The Committee became an asset to many senators. The complaints they received from constituents were forwarded to the Committee for investigation and senators often accompanied the Committee members on investigations in their home states. This was not only good public relations for the non-member senators, but once the Truman Committee was finished with its investigation, they became a valuable resource working with the proper local and federal authorities to solve the problems.

By establishing this framework, and given that it never accepted a bribe, the Committee was credible. Its organization and procedures had been well thought out, the goals and objectives were clear, and it was thorough and hardworking. Truman's efforts instilled self-confidence in the members, which soon blossomed into courage. They had the courage to question, to disagree and to recommend action against the leaders in business, government and the military.

Courage: No Fear to Investigate

In one of its first investigations, the Truman Committee had the courage to challenge governmental agency influence and big business interests in the aluminum industry. The Committee found and revealed gross selfish conduct by Alcoa (The Aluminum Company of America). The growing military conflicts in Europe and Asia required air power, and aluminum was a metal vital to the production of such aircraft. Alcoa produced virtually all the aluminum in America and in the Spring of 1941, the Truman Committee investigated the United States' capabilities to produce aluminum. The discoveries were shocking.

The Office of Production Management (OPM, an agency established by the Roosevelt administration to help organize the war mobilization effort) had relied on Alcoa for projections on the amount of aluminum that would be available for the war effort. Alcoa's figures had consistently shown an adequate supply and therefore the OPM "had said that talk of a shortage was misleading and that it was unpatriotic to talk about the possibility of such a shortage." Despite the efforts of Alcoa, in February of 1941 it became apparent that serious miscalculations had been made. Germany had the capacity to manufacture 915 million pounds of aluminum per year, and by 1943 it would be increased to nearly 1.4 billion pounds per year. In 1939, Alcoa's production capacity was 350 million pounds and in the ensuing year it had not made significant capacity increases.

As these deficiencies were brought to light, one of the key witnesses in the investigation was Jesse Jones, Jr., the Secretary of Commerce. He was responsible for negotiating a contract with Alcoa to expand processing plants. The pact, however, gave Alcoa a virtual monopoly over the aluminum industry while the government agreed to pay for the venture. As the investigation continued, Jones used his wealth of political influence to quell the Committee's efforts. Truman's Committee did not back down; Jones eventually testified and his questionable ethics were revealed. Later he agreed to renegotiate the contract. The Committee's report, critical of the OPM and condemning Alcoa, read in part:

1. The disclosures of the investigation brought to light that we are facing a serious shortage of aluminum and that we do not now have the capacity to overcome the deficiency.

2. . . . the Office of Production Management had apparently completely relied on (Alcoa) as a source of information as to the availability of aluminum and had discharged anyone else from going into the business of producing aluminum. Alcoa was at this time the only producer of aluminum in America. It is reasonable to conclude that Alcoa had convinced the Office of Production Management of the adequacy of supply in order to avoid the possibility that anyone else would go into a field which they had for so many years successfully monopolized.

3. Alcoa promised to build up its supply of bauxite but did not do so.

4. The demand (exceeded) the supply and in an effort to relieve the shortage the Office of Production Management issued priority regulations governing the distribution of aluminum to users. In the light of the serious shortage which exists, it is interesting to note that

substantial amounts of aluminum are still permitted to the automobile industry for use in production of pleasure cars.

5. At the time of the committee hearings the maximum capacity planned by the Office of Production Management was 800,000,000 pounds, of which 730,000,000 was to be produced by Alcoa.

Besides the inadequate supply of aluminum, another shortage which could render the United States vulnerable became visible. In addition to sufficient supplies of bauxite, aluminum manufacture required large amounts of electric power. One kilowatt of power was necessary for the production of 1000 pounds of aluminum. To meet the increased need for processed aluminum, additional power plants would need to be constructed. Alcoa had plans to build such a power plant in western North Carolina on the Little Tennessee River.

The Truman Committee's report exposed the selfish actions of Alcoa in this time of national emergency. It explained that the company filed for a federal license to build the plant, but Alcoa discovered that all such licenses would grant the government an option, after 50 years, to purchase the plant and reimburse the owners their legitimate investment. The report explained that Alcoa decided not to build the plant because it could not justify this potential risk to its stockholders.

The investigation also discovered that Alcoa had made agreements with I.G. Farben, a large German producer of metals. Alcoa had agreed not to produce magnesium (another metal vital to aircraft construction) and even sell Farben their supply at "prices far below those charged to American users of the metal." In return, Farben would not interfere in Alcoa's aluminum markets, which gave Alcoa a virtual monopoly at the expense of the U.S. war mobilization effort. This Truman Committee investigation exemplifies the courage that made it a valuable component in the effort to win the war.

A similar instance of courage was exhibited by the Committee in 1944 as they exposed waste, incompetence and thoughtlessness in the army and the War Department concerning the acquisition of a facility for a military hospital. On September 16, 1942, the Breakers Hotel in Palm Beach Florida was surveyed for the feasibility of conversion to an army hospital. The Breakers, owned by the Florida East Coast Hotel Company, was a nine-story luxury hotel with 500 rooms, "spacious grounds and considerable ocean frontage."

Further surveys were made on September 30 and November 20 without the army expressing interest in the property. But suddenly, on December 4, the army informed the owners that it was, in fact, interested, and on December 12, the army assumed possession. In addition to the $400,000-a-year lease, the army required $300,000 for the conversion to a hospital and similar figure would be needed for the conversion back to a hotel at the termination of the lease.

Conversion soon began and the hospital opened its doors on March 1, 1943. The Spring of 1943, however, witnessed a change in the war effort: the army reduced personnel in Florida and far fewer injured troops were transferred from the battle front to the United States for recovery. Consequently, the army decided it no longer required the facility. The hospital, after four months of use, had served only 661 patients at a cost of nearly $1 million. The United States surgeon general recommended that the facility be opened to attend to all American service personnel. On September 10, 1943 the surgeon general assumed jurisdiction over the facility which was renamed Ream General Hospital.

In mid-November, the undersecretary of war directed that all rental properties be surveyed and all real estate not needed be released. On January 8, 1944 the decision was made to abandon the facility but to use the hospital until September 1, 1944 at which time it would be reconverted to a hotel by December 10 for operations by the Florida East Coast Company.

The Truman Committee's conclusions were highly critical of the conduct of both the army and the War Department in the case of the Ream General Hospital. The report read in part:

1. The Breakers should never have been acquired.

2. The manner of acquisition, as in the case of other hotel properties in the Florida area, was high-handed and arbitrary.

3. The original decision to abandon the Breakers was made with insufficient consideration.

4. The reasons given for abandonment are not convincing. It appears that the property was abandoned because the War Department discovered it to have been a very poor original transaction, which resulted in a property which was bound to be too expensive.

5. Prior to March 31, 1943 there was no coordination of the hospital programs of the various agencies. As a result, the Breakers was acquired without consultation with any of the other agencies which might have been able to utilize excess army hospitals in suitable locations.

6. The War Department's statements of fact in connection with this entire matter do not appear to be accurate.

7. The War Department's principle reason for abandoning the Breakers Hotel appears to be the question of cost. Apparently the War Department's position on this subject have never been clear. It must originally have been thought that the cost would not be excessive. Otherwise it would not have determined to rent the hotel.

The Truman Committee's report exposed the facts and let blame fall where it should have. It did not dilute its conclusions because it was intimidated by the army and the War Department. The courage to release the findings to the public can be directly traced to the credibility the Committee had acquired by 1944.

By conservative estimates, the Special Senate Subcommittee to Investigate the National Defense Program saved taxpayers over $15 billion dollars and hundreds of lives. Considering the War Department's budget for fiscal year 1943 was just under $43 billion, the efforts of the Truman Committee were substantial. Despite the reports of incompetence, corruption and mismanagement, the Committee's efforts may have had a positive influence on the public's perception of the war effort; the Truman Committee was viewed by many as a cleansing agent. In most cases the injustices it discovered were corrected, which may have prevented others from taking advantage of the situation. The investigations may have caused other individuals, companies and agencies, fearing exposure, to adhere to the rules. These are unfortunate motives for ethical conduct, but often, that is the way it must be.

The success of the Committee had a positive effect on Truman's reputation. Prior to the investigations he was rumored to be an honest man because as Jackson County Judge, contractors and local politicians found him to be incorruptible. President Roosevelt asked Truman to run as vice president because, among other reasons, the effective and altruistic manner in which he operated his Committee had elevated his reputation to that of a man of the highest integrity.

Although its accomplishments are overshadowed by the events of World War II, and despite the fact that it is rarely mentioned in history books, the lesson of the Truman Committee still holds a major significance today. Nightly news broadcasts often briefly describe misuse or mismanagement of public funds. These reports are after the fact and merely scratch the surface. Americans are angered but little is done to prevent it from happening again. Look at our local and state governments, the Welfare program, Social Security and Medicare, the Defense Department, our national debt, and, most recently and tragically, the nation-wide savings and loan failures. What is perplexing about these travesties is that the American people have hawk-like vision concerning their personal finance. We carefully determine the best buy, the better percentage rate, the best investment and the most economical way to live our lives. So why, if the individual is concerned with personal expenditures, is not the government just as careful with the money it spends?

In terms of the "governmental net" analogy, Senator Truman was able to repair the damaged federal net before the issue of the war effort fell onto the mesh. After witnessing the greed and injustices of the 1980s, his motives for establishing the Committee are truly refreshing. His belief that the reason for holding a public office should be purely altruistic made his committee and his career successful. To fix our flawed nets, we are going to need leaders like Harry Truman, with integrity, a sense of foresight and courage to do the right thing in the face of corruption.

END OF WAR, TROUBLE BEGINS

April 12, 1945 had been another routine day of presiding over the Senate for Vice President Harry S. Truman. After he adjourned the Senate for the evening, he made his way to the office of House Speaker Sam Rayburn to discuss some bills on which the House and Senate were in disagreement. The vice president was looking forward to a relaxing evening of poker with a few old friends. When he arrived at the Speaker's office there was a message asking him to call the White House. Steve Early, President Roosevelt's Press Secretary, asked Mr. Truman to come to the White House immediately. Upon his arrival he was ushered to the second floor study where he greeted Mrs. Roosevelt.

"Harry," she said, "the President is dead." Soon Congressional leaders, government officials, and Bess and Margaret Truman had arrived at the White House. Once a Bible was found, Chief Justice Harlan Stone swore in Harry S. Truman as the 33rd President of the United States. Upon taking the oath of office, President Truman assumed an enormous responsibility. For the first time in 12 years, the nation was without the leader who had pulled the economy out of the Great Depression and was directing the allies to victory in mankind's most destructive war. In addition to inheriting the problems that Franklin Roosevelt had left, Truman had to heal the wounds of a mourning nation.

We've all felt the anxiety associated with a new job. Mr. Truman described his feelings to reporters on his first full day as president:

> Boys. . . if you ever pray, pray for me now. I don't know whether you fellows ever had a load of hay fall on you, but when they told me yesterday what had happened, I felt like the moon, stars, and all the

planets had fallen on me. I've got the most terribly responsible job a man ever had.

At this delicate time in history, the nation and free world looked to the United States for leadership. Truman's vision upon assuming the presidency was to establish peace and order to a war-torn and chaotic world. This meant that he would have to end the war as quickly as possible, attain an equitable solution with allied nations concerning the future status of Europe and save millions of Europeans from starvation in their devastated countries. To accomplish this, he relied on his decisive character.

Former President Richard Nixon expressed the importance of decisiveness in a leader: "Above all, he must be decisive. He must analyze his choices shrewdly and dispassionately, but then he must act. He must not become a Hamlet. He must not succumb to 'paralysis by analysis.'" Truman efficiently used the three stages of the decision-making process to make good, effective decisions:

1. **Perspective.** Truman learned all he could about the past and present of each situation. Because he read the available information, consulted advisors and experts, and drew upon his existing knowledge and experience, he had a thorough understanding of the who, what, when, why and where of the situation.

2. **Foresight.** Truman then looked to the future of the situation. He asked two principle questions: "How will my decision impact the future?" and "What are the pros and cons for each possible course of action?"

3. **Execution.** Truman made the decisions and then communicated them through the proper channels with poise, confidence and resolution.

Because Truman spent his time with these three stages, rarely did he have to engage in damage control. His decisions were well thought out and usually the best options available at the time.

The Atom Bomb

It is important to reiterate that the focus of this book is on the process and not on the political result of the leadership. Many of President Truman's decisions and policies were highly controversial. The moral and political correctness or incorrectness of his decision to use the atomic bomb against the Japanese at the end of World War II will be debated to eternity. My purpose is not to debate this issue—I will, however, assert that the process he used to gather the necessary information and predict possible outcomes is highly effective. Other persons in Truman's position may have chosen not to use the bomb, but if they used a decision making process similar to the president's, their decisions likely would have been successful. Thus, our study should be of the process and not the result.

The unprovoked and unexpected Japanese attack of Pearl Harbor in December 1941 was the spark that ignited American sentiment to enter World War II. Although the Japanese had dealt a major blow to the American navy, President Roosevelt believed it imperative to repel simultaneously the imperialistic Japanese and assist the European Allies. If the United States did not quickly reinforce Europe, the entire continent could have fallen to the Nazis. This left the burden of the conflict in the Pacific Theater to the United States. In early 1942, the Japanese Empire had conquered most of the Far East including the Philippines, Thailand, Korea and parts of China.

The United States rebounded from the destruction at Pearl Harbor to diminish the realm of Japanese influence to within their own islands by the end of 1943. Although the United States continued to bomb Tokyo and other strategic targets through 1945, many military experts explained that only an invasion of the Japanese Islands would be able to force the desired unconditional surrender. They predicted such an invasion would require at least 1 million American ground soldiers. Consequently, it could cost 500,000 of them their lives and would take an additional 12 to 18 months to achieve a surrender. Japanese forces would incur similar losses, and the battle would have been the bloodiest in world history. This was not acceptable to President Truman.

The evening Truman assumed the presidency, he was made aware of a new weapon that had destructive powers far beyond those of conventional armaments. The United States was very close to harnessing the power of nuclear fission in the form of the atomic bomb. Although it was still in the developmental stage, Truman formed "The Interim Committee" to make recommendations concerning nuclear policy to the president. It was composed of military officers, War Department officials and several scientists working on the project. The first test of the bomb was on July 16, 1945 in the desert near Alamagordo, New Mexico. The bomb was a complete success and it exceeded the expectations of even the scientists who built it. The official estimate was that its power would be equivalent to 5,000 pounds of TNT. The test explosion yielded a destructive power of 15,000 to 20,000 tons of TNT. Truman received this news at the Potsdam Conference in Europe where he was discussing plans for the reconstruction of Europe with Marshall Joseph Stalin of the Soviet Union and British Prime Minister Winston Churchill.

The situation President Truman faced was extremely complex—he had to resolve three serious problems. First, should he use the bomb and its awesome destructive force. Second, if he decided to use it, should it be used on targets within Japan (It was thought that the detonation of the device on a small uninhabited island might convince the Japanese to surrender). Finally, if he decided to drop it within Japan, which cities should be targeted for destruction and why. After he thoroughly understood these problems, he was ready to employ foresight to determine and eliminate options.

To solve the first problem, Truman weighed the loss of life for both an invasion and dropping the bomb. Sending hundreds of thousands of American soldiers to their death was unacceptable to the him. The Interim Committee recommended that the United States use the weapon as soon as possible. They further believed that no demonstration could be devised to show its destructive force adequately enough to force the Japanese to surrender.

The United States, working with Britain, took great care to keep the development of the bomb (termed the Manhattan Project) a secret. Truman asked Winston Churchill for his opinion on the use of the bomb against Japan. Churchill told Truman that if it could more quickly terminate the war, then he favored its use. Truman also, because it was such a monumental decision, sought the opinion of Stalin at the Potsdam Conference. Although Truman gave him few specifics of the bomb, Stalin did not show much interest in the project. Stalin did, though, advise the President to use it against the Japanese. Truman concluded that the employment of the bomb would save lives. He further reasoned that the world had endured five years of grueling war and that it was best to end the war as quickly as possible.

To solve the second problem, Truman decided to use the bomb against the Japanese rather than show its destructive force on a deserted island. Truman knew that dropping the bomb on the Japanese islands would result in the instantaneous death of thousands of Japanese soldiers and civilians, and a painful lingering death for the radiation-poisoned blast survivors. But Truman also knew that the Japanese believed it more honorable to die fighting than to surrender. The Japanese Air Force had many pilots volunteer to load their planes with explosives and crash into American naval vessels. These Kamakazis were not the only soldiers willing to give the ultimate sacrifice in the name of honor. In many battles, Japanese soldiers had to be burned out of tunnels and concrete machine gun pits. Many would even kill themselves with hand grenades rather than be captured by the Americans. This fanaticism convinced Truman that a display of the bomb's force would not be sufficient to force Japan to surrender.

Truman's decision that the bomb would be used on a Japanese city that was of military importance solved the third problem. Following the rules of war and the guidelines set at the Geneva Conventions, Truman was adamant about its use on a military target.

One such city was Kyoto, but he eliminated it from consideration because it was of cultural and religious importance to the Japanese. The field was narrowed to four cities and the first bomb was to be dropped after August 3 at a time and city to be determined by weather conditions. On August 6, 1945 an atomic blast devastated Hiroshima. The Japanese refusal to surrender precipitated a subsequent atomic explosion over Nagasaki three days later. On August 10, the Japanese surrendered to the allies. Even after the second bomb, many Japanese soldiers did not want to surrender, and a coup attempt was made to keep the Emperor from capitulating. As president of the United States, Truman shouldered the responsibility for the decision. "The final decision," said Truman, "of where and when to use the atomic bomb was up to me. Let there be no mistake about it. I regarded the bomb as a military weapon and never had any doubt that it should be used."

President Truman had consistently maintained that the United States was not at war with the people of Japan. Many times he asked a representative of the Japanese people, not the government, to step forward and negotiate a peace. Although the bomb would be dropped on a military target, it would kill thousands of civilians. Ideally, this was not the way to end the war. Realistically, an invasion was not the answer either. Although the ethics of his decision have been questioned, the results are clear. The war ended almost immediately with 190,000 further casualties compared to the estimates of one additional year of war and both sides incurring a total of 1 million casualties. Truman's critics who merely claim that he caused the death of nearly 200,000 Japanese civilians forget the loss of life, pain and suffering that would have been incurred by both sides had he ordered an invasion.

A Devastated Europe

Issues in the European Theater were much more difficult to solve. For five years, World War II ravaged Europe, but by the Spring of 1945, Mussolini was removed from power in Italy and General Patton's Third Army pushed the German Army back to within its own borders. Victory was within sight, but a prolonged effort by the allies to gain unconditional surrender meant loss of life for thousands of American soldiers. The Germans were willing to surrender to the United States and Great Britain, but were reluctant to include the Russians in the agreement. Heinrich Himmler, acting as German Head of State after the death of Adolph Hitler, believed that peace on the Western Front would allow Germany to continue to fight the Russians in the East. Truman and British Prime Minister Winston Churchill completely agreed that a German surrender would have to include the Soviets. They hoped that this would maintain the Allied front and help to avoid ill-feelings when peace negotiations began. The Germans agreed to the Allied terms of unconditional surrender, and hostilities ended at midnight May 8-9.

Once the fighting had ceased in Europe, countries scrambled to regain previously occupied territory. Often, however, those nations that had the military control of the area were reluctant to withdraw. This made the already precarious European situation even more delicate. French General Charles De Gaulle refused to withdraw from German territory, invaded Northern Italy and sent troops into Syria and Lebanon to reestablish French influence there. Truman and Churchill requested De Gaulle refrain from the imperialistic actions. Upon the general's refusal, President Truman decisively halted the shipping of guns, ammunition and supplies to the French. De Gaulle soon complied. Similar questions of territorial occupation and rightful ownership surfaced in Germany, Austria, Yugoslavia and Poland. Additionally, the entire world economy was demolished. Clearly, solving the problems of postwar Europe were going to require leadership. President Harry S. Truman delivered.

In an effort to resolve these problems, the Big Three, Truman, Churchill and Soviet Premiere Joseph Stalin arranged to meet in July, 1945. The meetings, known as the Potsdam Conference, were to be held in Berlin, Germany, but the devastation in that city was so great, the meetings were moved to the neighboring town of Potsdam. Truman explained his aspirations for the Conference: "I did not want to just discuss. I wanted to decide.

I was there to get something accomplished, and if we could not do that, I meant to go back home." Truman's decisiveness would be an asset to the Conference but as he would discover, it would not be enough to reach an equitable agreement on the future status of Europe.

The conference was officially called to order at 5:10 p.m. on July 17, 1945. Stalin motioned for President Truman to act as presiding officer and Churchill's second made it official. The first meeting set the agenda for the subsequent meetings. After this assembly, Truman put the Conference into perspective:

> I did not underestimate the difficulties before us. I realized that as chairman I would be faced with many problems arising out of the conflicts of interests. I knew that Stalin and Churchill each would have special interests that might clash and distract us . . . I knew that I was dealing with two men of entirely different temperaments, attitudes and backgrounds. Churchill was great in argument. His command of the spoken word is hard to equal. Stalin was not given to long speeches. He would reduce arguments quickly to the question of power and had little patience with any other kind of approach.

The Big Three discussed, debated and argued many issues, including the fate of the German naval and merchant fleet; what actions to take concerning the Franco regime in Spain; the status of free elections in Bulgaria, Rumania and Greece; the division of Germany; and the extent of war reparations to be paid to the Allies by the defeated nations. In July, Britain conducted national elections and Churchill's party was defeated; on July 28, Clement Atlee became the British Prime Minister. Because he had been present at all of the Potsdam meetings, cohesiveness was easy to maintain.

The agreements on war reparations, the division of Germany and the decision to try Nazi leaders as war criminals was greatly overshadowed by what Churchill described as a Soviet "Iron Curtain" falling across Eastern Europe. The Allies were unable to decide on the Eastern border of Poland and which government should be empowered there—the freely elected or the Soviet's choice. The reluctance of the Soviet Union to allow free elections in Poland was a preview of the oppression imposed on the satellite nations by the Soviet Union.

Truman was frustrated by the Conference. He was disappointed not only in the lack of agreement, but in his counterparts' indecisiveness. Complained Truman:

> I was getting very impatient, as I had many times before in these sessions, with all the repetition and beating around the bush, but I restrained myself. . . I did not see why they (Stalin, Churchill and Atlee) could not come right to the point and get it over with instead of doing so much talking.

It was vitally important for him to stifle this frustration with his comrades for an outward display would have soured the conference and caused ill-feelings between the Big Three. It would have eliminated the possibility of achieving even minor agreements and could have potentially fueled hostilities between the Allies. Despite his restraint, relations with the Soviets deteriorated and there was little Truman could do to prevent it. Truman described the cause of what would be the Cold War:

> Many differences among the Allies had been subordinated during the war, but now that the common enemy was defeated, the problems of peace had brought these differences to the surface. We had already discovered how difficult the Russians could be, but in the months that immediately followed the war this was revealed even further.

Truman's skill in forming a perspective and using foresight to reach a decision made the solutions in Europe obvious to the president, but getting the Soviets and British to decide and agree was becoming an impossibility. The difficulties at the conference were making it very clear that Truman's great skill and ability in decision making would not be sufficient to restore order to the world. And it was becoming evident to President Truman, as we recently have learned in the post-Gulf War Middle East, that despite the great power, influence and respect bestowed upon the president of the United States, there are still problems too large and complex for one man or one nation to solve.

Truman did all he could to prevent the situation from deteriorating further. He changed what aspects of the situation he could and then accepted that there were people, events and circumstances beyond his control. He channeled his negative feelings of disappointment and frustration into the positive energy of developing a plan to save and rebuild Western Europe.

The Marshall Plan

By June of 1947, tensions between the Western Allies and the Soviet Union had grown worse. The Iron Curtain had strengthened, and politically unstable countries throughout the world were targets for communist revolution. These new governments quickly allied themselves with the Soviet Union to gain protection and support. As in the case of Poland, they soon became "puppet regimes" of the Kremlin.

As the economies of most European nations had yet to recover from the war, they were at risk to communist subjection. The winter of 1947 was extremely harsh. Millions of people were starving across Europe, and the United States was the only country with the resources to help. Britain was broke and France was still recovering. This politically unstable posture of a starving and freezing Europe presented a danger to the balance of world power. President Truman foresaw a communist Europe as a threat not only to world security but to its economic recovery as well. Because of Cold War tensions, it's doubtful that a communist Europe would have traded with the United States. Truman reasoned that trade restrictions would create a very small market for American goods and cripple the economy.

It was becoming quite apparent to Truman that only American aid to Europe was going to save the situation. On June 5, 1947 Secretary of State General George Marshall, in an acceptance speech for an honorary degree from Harvard University, outlined the framework of what was to be called the Marshall Plan. It stipulated that the Europeans would work out the details of distribution while the United States would supply the money, materials and technical advice in a combined effort to restore the economies and living conditions in Europe.

Truman was very eager to give Marshall the credit for the plan for two reasons. First, he believed the plan would gain more support from Congress bearing the general's name. Truman's policies were becoming controversial and he did not want to risk the success of the program by taking credit. Second, Truman was very appreciative of the general's contributions to the government and to world peace. He believed Marshall should gain the recognition he deserved for his devotion to his country. Truman's prowess as a man of action was never more evident.

President Truman knew the $16 billion package would be met with much skepticism. He described the plan to House Speaker Rayburn, who would be instrumental in its passage through Congress. Truman explained that the consequences of inaction by the United States would include hundreds of thousands of Europeans starving and freezing to death, and a deep economic depression, first in Europe and then spreading to the United States. The Marshall Plan was approved by nearly a three-to-one margin by both houses of Congress. It worked very well, saving Europe from starvation, death and from falling behind the Iron Curtain. Predictably, however, the Soviets denounced the plan.

It has been argued by many historians that President Truman was responsible for the Cold War with the Soviets. On the contrary, Truman did everything possible to prevent it. Once the battle lines were drawn, he prevented the Cold War from resulting in military conflict. The Soviets were bent on imperialism following World War II, and Potsdam showed there was nothing Truman, Churchill or Atlee could do to persuade them otherwise. Although the Marshall Plan further polarized the conflict, Truman's other option was appeasement, which likely would have precipitated the collapse of Europe to communism, and eventually, a third world war.

Harry S. Truman stepped into "the most terribly responsible job a man ever had" and performed admirably. His leadership was responsible for the swift end to the war with Japan, the prevention of a third world war and a reconstructed Europe under the Marshall Plan. The United States was blessed by the leadership of Harry S. Truman at such a pivotal time in history.

THE KOREAN DECISIONS

Secretary of State Dean Acheson called President Truman at his home in Independence, Missouri, just after 10 p.m. on June 24, 1950.

"Mr. President," he said, "I have some very serious news. The North Koreans have invaded South Korea." This was not just another border-skirmish; the Communist North Korean People's Army (NKPA) was pouring over the 38th parallel into the Republic of Korea in large numbers at many points along the border. Concurrent to the invasion, the North Koreans broadcast a virtual declaration of war.

After World War II, Korea, liberated by the allies from Japan, was placed in a trusteeship. For convenience, the Soviet Union occupied Korean territory north of the 38th parallel and the United States occupied all territory south of the parallel. This trusteeship was designed to help restore self-governance to the Korean people and to establish free elections. Later in 1946 and 1947 the Soviets boycotted United Nations' actions that would have accomplished those goals. By 1950, the United States had turned governmental control over to the Koreans and the 38th parallel became the border between communism in the north and free republic in the south.

Time was not on Truman's side. As he and his staff gathered information and discussed options, the NKPA was advancing on the capital, Seoul, and cutting the South Koreans to

ribbons in the process. Within 48 hours of the invasion, President
Rhee was forced to move his South Korean government 150 miles
south to the town of Taegu. Truman had to act quickly if he was to
save Korea, but he needed information of both the invasion and of
U.S. capabilities in the region.

Before he could order extensive military action, he needed to
inform the Congressional leadership of the situation and ask for their
suggestions, comments and ultimately, their support. Truman knew
he would need the backing of Congress in the future as he was
going to need more troops, weapons and supplies from the
legislative branch to halt this and any other communist aggression.

This crisis, precipitated by the communists, could not have
come at a worse time for President Truman. Senator Joseph
McCarthy was at the height of his career, articulating his fervent
anti-communist sentiments. McCarthy preached that if you were
soft on communism, then you must be a communist yourself. Any
action, thought or implication of communist sympathy was met by
the demagogue with a verbal condemnation and call for appropriate
action. Millions of Americans were caught up in this "red scare"
while thousands faced public disgrace and lost their jobs to the
black-listing. The influence of McCarthyism only toughened
Truman's situation, and would make his decisions more
controversial with the frothing American public.

President Truman's decisiveness was the key to the success
of the American involvement in the Korean War. Without a strong
and thoughtful leader in the White House, the result of the
communist invasion into the free Republic of Korea most likely
would have been a third world war.

Quick Decisions

Truman's first decisions were to have the commander of the
Pacific fleet, General Douglas MacArthur, evacuate American
civilians from Korea, get ammunition and supplies to the retreating
South Korean Army, to survey the damage to the South Korean
Army and assess the advancement of the North Koreans. Once

completed, MacArthur reported to Truman that the South Koreans were unable to stop the advancing NKPA. The general also indicated that a complete collapse of the South Korean Army was imminent.

To form his perspective on the Korean situation, Truman relied on the information and opinions of his advisors and the military reports. He also utilized his vast wealth of historical knowledge about the Far East and found historical precedents which shed a different light on the situation. He complimented this knowledge with good, plain common sense.

Although the crisis had become a major international issue with hundreds of complex reports and details, he was able to sort through it and keep the situation in perspective. Truman's Secretary of State Dean Acheson noted this quality in the president:

> Mr. Truman was unable to make the simple complex in the way so many men in public life tend to do. For very understandable reasons, of course . . . if one makes something complex out of something simple, then one is able to delay making up one's mind. And that was something that never troubled Mr. Truman.

One reason Truman could quickly and accurately form a valid perspective was the efficient structure of his administration. It was organized to allow facts, thoughts, ideas and opinions to quickly reach the president. Importantly, Trumans' communicative process was to first understand the information and various opinions. Then and only then, did he communicate his decisions and plans of action.

Another reason he excelled in forming a perspective was that he possessed an unquenchable thirst for reading and learning history. He was able to see how the events of history fit together and that its cause-effect relationships are continual. He did this quite easily as new events happened—he just placed them within his existing framework of historical knowledge.

Once he gathered the necessary information and sorted it properly, he stated his perspective of the situation:

> There was now no doubt. The Republic of Korea needed help at once if it was not to be overrun. More seriously, a Communist success in Korea would put Red troops and planes within easy striking distance of Japan, and Okinawa and Formosa would be open from attack on two sides.
>
> I told my advisors that what was developing in Korea seemed to me like a repetition on a larger scale of what had happened in Berlin. The Reds were probing for weakness in our armor; we had to meet their thrust without getting involved in a world-wide war.

This statement is a perfect example of Truman's decision making process in action. He outlined his perspective of the situation in the first paragraph and used that understanding to employ foresight in the second. In his *Memoirs,* he reflected on his use of foresight:

> Every decision I made in connection with the Korean conflict had this in mind: to prevent a third world war and the terrible destruction it would bring to the civilized world. This meant we would not do anything that would provide the excuse to the Soviets and plunge the free nations into full-scale all-out war. I could not agree with the tactics or approach of those who, like Chaing Kai-shek in a speech on July 3, 1950, wanted the U.N. to charge the Russians with the full responsibility for this Korean conflict and to demand that Moscow put an end to it. This kind of bluster is certain to lead into an impossible dilemma.

President Truman did not want his solution to cause new and more dangerous problems. Now he was between the proverbial rock and a hard place. If he did not take action, it gave the communists a victory and a strategic stronghold in an unsettled Far East and set a precedent of American softness on communism which could have eventually led to war in Europe. If he acted too brashly, he could find himself in a nuclear exchange with the Soviets.

Although not of this magnitude, most of us have at some point in our life, been called on in a position of responsibility to solve a potentially dangerous situation. With this burden, we have felt that despair of finding ourselves, as Truman did, in a veritable catch-22 situation. Although he had the fate of the world resting on his back, Truman had to shunt those feelings of frustration and despair and determine an appropriate course of action. Truman's ability to parlay knowledge and experience into a sense of foresight funnelled his thoughts directly to the place they needed to be: finding a solution. He did not spend an inordinate amount of time with the problem. In short, the president had to find a solution that would repel the communist invasion but would not cause an all-out war.

Truman and his staff decided it was important to involve the United Nations in the denouncement of the aggression and to include them in the solution of the crisis. This would insure that it was not the United States acting alone against the communists. Truman knew that it was imperative to gain international support; world opinion in his corner reduced the threat of overt Soviet intervention on the side of the North Koreans. Truman (via Secretary of State Dean Acheson) asked for a Security Council meeting of the United Nations to condemn the aggression and ask for a cease-fire.

By a vote of 9 to 0, the United Nations Security Council, (absent the boycotting Soviet delegation) approved a declaration that the North Korean action was a "breach of the peace" established by the United Nations at the conclusion of World War II. The measure also ordered the North Koreans to stop the aggression and to withdraw from the Republic of Korea.

In August and September of 1990, President George Bush's successful efforts to assemble an international coalition to oppose the invasion of Kuwait by Iraq closely resembles Truman's efforts in Korea. Bush quickly asked for action by the United Nations and sent Secretary of State James Baker, globe trotting to solicit international support. Unlike Truman however, Bush had the support of the Soviet Union; in 1950 the Soviets caused the crisis.

Truman ordered U.S. air and naval forces to support the ROK forces on June 27, but the surging NKPA invasion was too organized and powerful. The following day, Seoul fell to the communists. On July 8, Truman named General Douglas MacArthur as the head of the United Nations command in Korea. Contrary to the earlier pleas of President Truman and Commander of the Allied Troops General Dwight Eisenhower, the United States Congress had drastically scaled down the armed forces in the five years since the end of World War II. The U.S. Armed Services would be facing a manpower shortage if this was to be an extended endeavor.

MacArthur reported that the only way to save the situation would be to deploy U.S. ground troops. Truman did not want to see a communist South Korea but he did not want to over-commit his troops in Korea leaving Europe open to further communist aggression. Truman now faced a very big decision. Ideally, he would have liked to rid Korea and the Far East of communism. McCarthy and his supporters would have been in favor of such a notion. Realistically, however, to do that, Truman would have had to commit the United States to a third world war. Chairman of the Joint Chiefs of Staff, Omar Bradley had said that an all-out war in this situation "would be the wrong war at the wrong place at the wrong time with the wrong enemy."

President Truman believed the Soviets were testing the commitment of the United States to repel communism and that Korea could be a trap to catch the United States over-extending its forces in the Far East. This would leave Europe, still recovering under the Marshall Plan, open for further communist aggression.

Truman's decision to escalate American involvement by pledging ground troops in the Korean conflict was a big one indeed. With it came the possibility of Soviet involvement and a third world war. For if even a Soviet advisor to the NKPA had been killed, it would have given the Soviets an excuse to either retaliate, possibly in Europe, or to enter the Korean conflict. After consultation with advisors, Truman gave MacArthur the use of the ground troops under his command to repel the NKPA invasion.

Despite the U.N. sanctions, the South Korean Army was forced south almost off the peninsula before American troops could arrive. It was going to take a prolonged effort to drive back the communists and restore the order that preceded the invasion.

The Chinese Nationalists, under the command of Generalisimo Chaing Kai-shek, offered 30,000 of their "best" troops to repel the communist attack. President Truman sent MacArthur to Formosa to inform Chaing Kai-shek that the use of his troops "would be inappropriate." Truman and MacArthur were in agreement that the 30,000 poorly-trained and ill-equipped troops Chaing had to offer would be more of a burden than an asset in Korea. Furthermore, Truman believed, with Chaing's troops in Korea, Formosa would be left open to attack from the communist Chinese.

After the conference, Chaing announced that he and General MacArthur were in "total agreement" and that Chaing's army should not be used in Korea, but they should be "unleashed" directly into the Chinese mainland. MacArthur denied that he had communicated that position to Chaing. Truman sent his trusted advisor, Averell Harriman, to meet the general and to clear up the misunderstanding.

By mid-July, the allied forces numbered 75,000 men composed of 18,000 Americans. On July 20, Teajon was captured by the NKPA. But the tide was beginning to turn. In August the U.N. forces were fully organized and were in sufficient numbers to begin an offensive. Congress removed the limitations on the size of the United States Army and British forces arrived in Korea.

At the end of August, Truman and MacArthur had another "misunderstanding." MacArthur sent a letter to the commander in chief of the Veterans of Foreign Wars which outlined his assessment of the Far Eastern situation. It was, however, in complete contradiction to the policies of the Truman administration. MacArthur advocated escalation of the conflict to include fighting north of the 38th parallel rather than the Truman policy to "reduce the area of conflict in the Far East." Because the letter was printed in various magazines and newspapers, it sent conflicting signals to the American public and to the allied nations as to the actual position of the United States in the Far East conflict. MacArthur, at Truman's direction, withdrew the statement. Said Truman:

> I would never deny General MacArthur or anyone else the right to differ with me in opinions. The official position of the United States, however, is defined by decisions and declarations of the President. There can be only one voice in stating the position of this country in the field of foreign relations.

Although MacArthur's method was inappropriate, it shows Truman's almost unquenchable thirst for opinions and information about a given situation. It also demonstrates how efficient his style of communication was. Again, this was a major factor in Truman's ability to make good decisions quickly. By continually looking for new and additional information, he was able to alter his perspective as the situation changed.

In spite of his dissenting views of how the war should be fought, MacArthur's strategic brilliance was changing the course of the war. By September 15, the allied forces had recaptured Inchon and two weeks later General MacArthur returned Seoul to ROK President Rhee. The effort was becoming a United Nations force rather than solely an action of the United States; 16 nations had deployed troops under the U.N. command.

As Allied troops neared the 38th parallel, the threat of Chinese intervention became greater. Truman wanted to communicate his policies directly to the general so there would be no further misunderstandings which could drag the Chinese into the conflict. Truman scheduled a conference on Wake Island in the Pacific for October 15, 1950. Truman had two reasons for arranging a meeting. First, because he and the general had never met, Truman thought that a personal contact might help to iron out some of their problems. Second, at this pivotal time in the conflict, Truman thought it necessary to get information from the general himself. The lines of communication between Washington and the Far East were efficient for the day, but they did not allow for a secure conversation. As well as provide the latest information, a face-to-face talk with MacArthur would afford Truman the details privilege only to those close to the action.

Since MacArthur had served in the Far East for the preceding 14 years, he had an expert knowledge of the overall Far East situation. By obtaining this valuable information, Truman was able to make decisions that would better solve the problems involving this and other potential communist aggression in the Far East.

President Truman and General MacArthur spent about an hour alone talking of the war on the morning of October 15 on Wake Island. The general made two major predictions during this meeting with his boss. First, MacArthur assured the president that victory was won in Korea, that all resistance would end by Thanksgiving and most of the troops could be sent back to bases in Germany by the first of the year. Second, MacArthur predicted that the Chinese communists would not enter the conflict.

Truman was pleased with the progress of the allied troops but he wanted to reiterate to his general the United States' Foreign Policy of a limited war in Korea. He did not want to engage the Chinese Communists or the Soviets or to provoke them into entering the conflict. This was a hard concept for MacArthur to understand. He had never fought in anything less than an all-out war where the objectives were to make the enemy give an unconditional surrender. Having stated his position face to face, Truman was satisfied that MacArthur understood the policy of the United States in the Far East.

As Truman and MacArthur discussed the situation, the flavor of the war was to change forever. Unbeknownst to the allies, Red (communist) Chinese Premier Mao Tse-tung decided to intervene in the conflict. By mid-October over 120,000 Red Chinese troops had covertly joined the NKPA. Before they had a chance to be fully organized within the ranks, the U.N. forces were driving north toward the Chinese border. Truman gave the okay to engage the Chinese Communist Forces (CCF) but allied troops were under no circumstances to cross the Yalu River into Chinese territory. The president believed an attack on the Red Chinese within their own borders would have precipitated their all-out involvement in the conflict.

As the CCF troops were incorporated into the NKPA strategy, the tide again changed. With the addition of hundreds of thousands of Chinese troops, the much larger communist army drove the allied forces out of Seoul and Inchon by the end of 1950. Both of MacArthur's predictions had been wrong: The fighting was far from over and the Red Chinese had entered the war.

The General Must Go

With the allied retreat came MacArthur's excuses for the failure. The general became highly critical of Truman's policies and decisions. He blamed the allied troubles on the orders from Washington to limit the hostilities in Korea. Again, Truman did not want to bomb strategic targets within the Chinese border because it would have not only violated U.N. directives, but it would have given the Chinese every reason to make a full-scale entry into the war. Furthermore, the Chinese had a pact with the Soviets which would have committed Soviet troops if the allies attacked China.

From experience, Truman was aware that commanding officers in each theater of a war believe they are at the greatest risk from attack and therefore need more attention, troops and equipment. Always the student of history, Truman noted:

> When I was in command of Battery D in World War I, that was the center of the war effort for me, and I could and did argue with the battalion staff for always more and better equipment and attention for my outfit. As Senator, my investigations had given me an insight to the constant contest between the war theaters for the lion's share of the war production, and as President, I always tried to listen to all sides before approving what I thought was the most balanced approach.

MacArthur believed that Asia should get the bulk of the American supplies, troops and attention. In addition, he believed his policy of a total United States commitment to the Far East was the only way to save Europe from the communists. His logic followed that if Asia fell to the communists, Europe would too. Therefore, he believed the United States should engage and defeat Red China. Truman, able to see and understand the larger picture, thought that a total commitment in the Far East would *cause* a communist invasion in Europe, not prevent it.

MacArthur soon made public his skepticism of Truman's policies. Because there could be only one voice stating United States Foreign Policy, President Truman, on December 5, 1950, issued a directive that no public statement should be made concerning foreign policy unless it was cleared first by the State Department. This, Truman hoped, would prevent MacArthur from misrepresenting the commitments and intentions of the United States.

Senator McCarthy's anti-communist discourse helped persuade a majority of Americans to oppose to the administration's policies in the Far East. Additionally, the press labeled the conflict "Truman's War." The president was losing support in both Houses of Congress including fellow Democrats. This lack of faith in his administration did not bother the president. Truman was convinced that his course of action was correct and that he was following the only path that would prevent a third world war.

On March 24, 1951 General MacArthur released a statement that, in effect, gave the Chinese an ultimatum. The statement hinted that the full power of the allied forces might be directed against Red China. This was in direct conflict with the Truman administration's policies and the messages it had been sending to the allies and the United Nations. The result was total confusion among the allies. Truman received a flood of inquiries from governments all over the world asking if the United States was still commited to the United Nations-sanctioned actions or if the president planned to escalate the conflict. MacArthur's statement was also insubordinate of Truman's December 5 directive that no foreign policy statement be released without prior consent of the State Department.

Truman's reaction was one of surprise:

I can only say that on that day I was deeply shocked. I had never underestimated my difficulties with MacArthur, but after the Wake Island meeting I had hoped that he would respect the authority of the President. I tried to place myself in his position, however, and tried to figure out why he was challenging the traditional civilian supremacy in our government.

Certainly his arguments and proposals had always received full consideration by me and the Joint Chiefs of Staff. If anything, they— and I—had leaned over backward in our respect for the man's military reputation.

President Truman looked to his great wealth of historical knowledge to find a parallel in his situation—President Abraham Lincoln and his plight with General George B. McClellan during the Civil War. Truman knew from Lincoln's experience with an insubordinate general, there was no choice but to relieve the commander.

Mr. Truman defined in his *Memoirs* the situation he faced:

I have always had, and have to this day, the greatest respect for General MacArthur, the soldier. Nothing I could do, I knew, could change his stature as one of the outstanding military figures of our time—and I had no desire to diminish his stature. I had hoped, and I had tried to convince him, that the policy he was asked to follow was right. He had disagreed. He had openly been critical. Now, at last, his actions had frustrated a political course decided upon, in conjunction with its allies, by the government he was sworn to serve. If I allowed him to defy the civil authorities in this manner, I myself would be violating my oath to uphold and defend the Constitution.

In addition to this public statement, MacArthur wrote a letter to House minority leader Joseph W. Martin which was highly critical of the Truman administration's policies—in effect he stated that they were illogical and violated American tradition. The *coup de grace* against MacArthur in the eyes of Truman was when Representative Martin read the letter to the House on April 5. But, before acting rashly in a moment of rage, Truman asked his cabinet and the Joint Chiefs of Staff to review the actions and statements of General MacArthur and recommend a course of action.

The president was sure of the course of action he was to take—he was going to relieve the general of command, but he wanted to hear additional points of view so he could better defend the decision. He wanted their opinions on the ramifications the firing would have upon Congress, the allies and the American public. On the morning of April 11, 1951, President Truman relieved General MacArthur of his command and replaced him with General Ridgeway.

Truman tried to execute his decision through the proper channels. He planned to have Acheson send the message to U.S. Ambassador Muccio in Korea who would deliver the orders to Secretary of the Army, General Frank Pace. Pace was then to deliver the orders to General MacArthur himself. But Pace was touring the front lines and unable to be contacted. Truman also believed that the news of the firing had been leaked to the press. He then decided to send the orders directly to MacArthur so that he would not learn the news first from the press. Once the general received his orders, President Truman held a press conference detailing the events. Truman handled the execution of this delicate situation very well. If the press had announced the news before MacArthur had been informed it would have caused an even greater controversy and been an embarrassment to Truman, MacArthur and to the army.

His decision to relieve MacArthur was not popular with the American public or with the Congress. MacArthur returned to the United States to a hero's welcome. He was treated to a ticker-tape parade in New York City on April 20, and he addressed a joint session of Congress with his "Old soldiers never die . . . they just fade away" speech. The event had the predictable but unfortunate effect of drawing public attention away from the Korean War and focusing it on the personal disagreements between the Commander in Chief and his general.

On July, 1 the NKPA and CCF agreed to armistice talks with the U.N. forces but they progressed very slowly. Fighting was still going on and each side would frequently boycott the talks. The 38th parallel had become the battle line and it was not until June of 1953 that an armistice was agreed upon.

Many are highly critical of Truman concerning his concept of a limited war in Korea and for his dismissal of the popular General MacArthur. But, for each decision he made, Truman was well informed. He relied on his advisors, military reports, his extensive historical knowledge and plain common sense to form his perspective. His ability to understand the continual cause-effect relationship of the past, present and future fostered a sense of foresight which made the decisions more successful and easier to make. President Truman commented on the value of foresight to a leader:

> As I look at some of the great decisions of the past, I am inclined to believe that the leaders who made them possessed and almost intuitive sense of the future. Their greatness lay in the fact that they could see further ahead than any of their contemporaries.

Truman's ability to balance the idealistic and the realistic made it possible to find solutions to the Korean conflict which would avert a third world war. After witnessing some of the bungled events and tragedies of the late twentieth century, its easy to conclude that many of our elected officials and business executives can learn a great deal about a vision, decisiveness and integrity from Harry S. Truman.

By examining the significant periods throughout his life, it is very evident that Truman learned from the past. The examples of decisiveness he exhibited during the Korean crisis illustrate how those abilities matured since assuming the presidency in 1945. His courage was a refinement of those qualities employed during the Truman Committee hearings. President Truman's conduct during the Korean crisis was the work of a seasoned veteran using the knowledge and skills he learned throughout his adult life.

From a Lieutenant grappling with the unruly Battery D in 1917 to the president who relieved General MacArthur in 1951, America was blessed with a model of the integrity and a competency so vital for a public official. America of the 1930s, 1940s and 1950s was fortunate to have a man of such character serving the public.

If we stop for a moment to study our own local, state and national governments, it would appear that we again need some men and women in politics that have Truman's integrity and altruistic view of public service so that they may begin to repair our damaged governmental nets. These are three of the qualities that each of us should be looking for in our business and political hopefuls of today.

In Merle Miller's *Plain Speaking*, President Truman evaluated his life and career:

> I grew up wanting to be as good a man as my father was and my mother wanted me to be. I never had the notion that I was anything special at all; even when I got that job in the White House, I didn't. And I never had the notion that there weren't a lot of people who couldn't do whatever it was better than I could.
>
> But that never worried me. All that ever concerned me was that I wanted to do the best I could. So I guess I'd have to say to that, to your question, that I always tried to be satisfied with what I was and what I was doing. My father used to say that a man ought to leave the world a little better than it was when he came into it, and if that can be said about me, I guess you'll have to say I lived a successful life.

Chapter 3

John F. Kennedy

Never has a single family dominated American politics in the way the Kennedys did in the late 1950s and early 1960s. In 1956, John (Jack) Kennedy was a senator from Massachusetts and narrowly missed the Democratic nomination for vice-president. Robert (Bobby) F. Kennedy had served as legal counsel on many House and Senate committees including the infamous Senate Permanent Investigations subcommittee chaired by communist hunter Joseph McCarthy. By 1962, John was president, Bobby was the attorney general, brother Ted represented Massachusetts in the Senate and brother-in-law Robert Sargent Shriver, Jr. was Director of the Peace Corps.

The family's attraction to politics dates back to before the turn of the century when John Kennedy's maternal and paternal grandfathers were public officials in Boston. John F. Fitzgerald was the mayor of Boston and Patrick Joseph Kennedy was a state representative and later a state senator. Although they were often political allies, they disliked each other personally. In 1914 however, Joseph P. Kennedy married Rose Fitzgerald and the two fathers eventually shared nine grandchildren.

Joseph Kennedy had great influence over his children. He stressed a competitiveness that became the way of life for the Kennedy children. He also became quite wealthy and was able to provide everything for them. On his sixth birthday, John Kennedy received a trust fund worth $1 million. The Kennedy fortune, estimated in 1957 between $200 and $400 million, came from many sources. Joe was a shrewd businessman in real estate and "playing" the stock market. Kennedy and his associates would buy cheap stocks and inflate the price through rumors. Investors, believing Kennedy's group was attempting a takeover, would purchase the stock, further inflating the stock's value. Once the price was sufficiently inflated, the group would sell their shares for enormous profits.

Joe Kennedy's wealth was his telling feature, but he had political ambitions as well. In 1934 President Roosevelt appointed him as the first director of the Securities and Exchange Commission. One of his first actions was to make the practices of rumors in the stock market, by which he made his fortune, illegal. In 1938 FDR appointed Kennedy as the ambassador to England. From there Kennedy hoped to get Roosevelt's support for the presidency in 1940, but the incumbent decided to run for a third term, which eventually led to a falling out between the two. With his hopes of occupying the Oval Office dashed, Joe Kennedy focused his efforts to place a family member there.

Joseph P. Kennedy, Jr. was the eldest of the Kennedy children and had a bright future in politics. He attended Harvard where he was a standout athlete. He received his law degree and became a naval pilot as the war in Europe grew. His life came to a tragic end in 1944 while flying a secret mission to bomb Germany. The plane suddenly exploded after take-off and his body was never found. The role of politician then fell on the next eldest son—Jack.

John Kennedy had difficulty staying healthy as a child. He had scarlet fever, jaundice, hepatitis and an appendicitis all before the age of 20. After graduating from prep school, John, like Joe, Jr. attended Harvard. Jack, however, felt lost in the shadow of his popular brother. Jack joined the football team but because he was frail for a football player (six feet tall but only 160 pounds) and unable to gain weight, he played on the junior varsity team. His serious back injury, which would plague him throughout life, was inflicted while playing football. His grades were average in school but he was not interested in many of the subjects. Through the help of his father, his senior thesis was published, *Why England Slept*, which gained international recognition.

Upon graduation, Jack could not decided on a career to pursue. He joined the navy and eventually was the commander of the PT-109 in the Pacific fleet. In August of 1943 his craft was rammed and sunk by a Japanese destroyer. Kennedy, with an injured sailor in tow, and his crew swam three miles to the nearest island. The island was uninhabited and the young PT commander swam to other nearby islands looking for help. For his heroic efforts, Kennedy was awarded the Navy and Marine Corps Medal. The ordeal re-injured his back and he underwent corrective surgery and was discharged from the navy in 1945.

Later that year he became a newspaper correspondent but said he did not care much for journalism because it was not an active occupation. He felt that instead of making things happen, journalists reactively wrote about the people who made things happen. At the urging of the his father, John F. Kennedy began his political career as one of nine Democratic candidates for Congress in the 11th district of Massachusetts. He was quite an underdog and some politicians even laughed when the 29 year-old announced his candidacy.

The entire Kennedy clan mobilized in the effort to send Jack to Washington. The family members went from door to door shaking hands, kissing babies and urging voters to vote for Jack. The Kennedy women arranged house parties throughout the district. The Kennedy's supplied all the necessities—flowers, cookies, pastries, tea, coffee, china and silverware. These efforts, made possible by the Kennedy wealth, proved fruitful as Kennedy was elected to represent the 11th district. After his third term in the House, Kennedy turned his eyes toward the Senate seat of Republican Henry Cabot Lodge, Jr. Kennedy, again the underdog, with the help of his family, was successful in the November election.

Kennedy's achievements during his eight years in the Senate were not of a legislative nature. In 1953 John F. Kennedy married Jaqueline Bouvier. In 1956 recovering from another back surgery, he wrote the Pulitzer Prize-winning book, *Profiles in Courage* . He had a rather lackadaisical approach to legislative business. Senators often remarked at Kennedy's frequent absence from votes and committee meetings. For the same reason he disliked journalism, he was frustrated and bored with legislative politics; Congress debated, discussed and appropriated—the Executive branch took the action. Despite his minimal legislative accomplishments, Kennedy was popular.

In 1956 Estes Kefauver edged out Kennedy as the Democratic nominee for vice president on the ticket with Adlai Stevenson. The Democrats were crushed in the elections that year. Had Kennedy been on the ticket, he likely would have been blamed for the loss because he was a Catholic. In 1928 Al Smith, a Catholic was soundly defeated by Herbert Hoover and the loss was blamed on Smith's Catholicism. It is highly probable that had Kennedy not fallen short in 1956, the inevitable Eisenhower landslide would have dashed all of his presidential aspirations. However, Kennedy hoped to parlay the attention he received in 1956 into the Democratic presidential nomination in 1960.

John Kennedy started campaigning much earlier than his opponents in all of his election campaigns. Although he formally announced his intentions on January 3, 1960, Kennedy was preparing for his candidacy in 1958. In his Senate reelection that year he particularly attacked the Eisenhower administration. He also had been giving a number of speeches in the South laying the groundwork for its support in 1960.

Hubert Humphry was the only national candidate that challenged Kennedy in the Democratic primaries in 1960. Kennedy defeated Humphry in the Wisconsin primary, but Humphry decided to challenge the Catholic candidate in West Virginia—a state that was 95 percent Protestant. Kennedy decided to confront the religious issue. He told his audiences that nobody had asked the two Kennedy brothers whether or not they were Catholics when they volunteered for military service. He explained that he did not believe that his brother had died for a bigoted country that would deny a Catholic the presidency. On the May 10 election day, Kennedy received 220,000 votes to Humphry's 142,000. This victory proved to Democrats and the national voting audience that indeed his candidacy should be taken seriously. Later that summer, Kennedy won the Democratic nomination and chose Senate Majority Leader Lyndon Johnson as his running mate.

Kennedy wanted to part with the "false prosperity" of the 1950s under President Dwight Eisenhower where a majority of Americans were happy but very little was accomplished. John Kennedy's strength as a leader lay in his ability to form a desirable vision of the future, communicate it to America and to help execute it. In his acceptance speech for the Democratic nomination on July 15, 1960, Kennedy introduced his plan for America:

> . . . the problems are not all solved and the battles are not all won—and we stand today on the edge of a New Frontier--the frontier of the 1960's—a frontier of unknown opportunities and perils—a frontier of unknown hopes and threats.
>
> Woodrow Wilson's New freedom promised our nation a new political and economic framework. Franklin Roosevelt's New Deal promised security and succor to those in need. But the New Frontier of which I speak is not a set of promises—it is a set of challenges. It sums up not what I intend to offer the American people, but what I intend to ask of them. It appeals to their pride, not to their pocketbook--it holds out the promise of more sacrifice instead of more security.
>
> But I tell you the New Frontier is here, whether we seek it or not. Beyond that frontier are the uncharted areas of science and space, unsolved problems of peace and war, unconquered pockets of ignorance and prejudice, unanswered questions of poverty and surplus. It would be easier to shrink back from that frontier, to look to the safe mediocrity of the past, to be lulled by good intentions and high rhetoric. . .
>
> Are we up to the task—are we equal to the challenge? Are we willing to match the Russian sacrifice of the present for the future—or must we sacrifice our future to enjoy the present?
>
> That is the question of the New Frontier. That is the choice our nation must make—a choice that lies not merely between two men or two parties, but between the public interest and private comfort— between national greatness and national decline—between the fresh air of progress and the stale, dank atmosphere of "normalcy"—between determined dedication and creeping mediocrity.

. . . I believe the times demand invention, innovation, imagination, decision. I am asking each of you to be new pioneers on that New Frontier.

Kennedy's opponents were Vice President Richard Nixon and Henry Cabot Lodge, Jr. In the nation's first televised debate Kennedy was opposing the man who had been vice president for eight years, debated Khrushchev and had sent Alger Hiss to prison. But the young senator exuded confidence, poise and resolution while explaining his position on the issues. The polls consistently showed Nixon with a lead, but as election day approached, Kennedy's support was growing. Although the senator won the popular vote by the slim margin of 118,000 votes, the electorial vote was decidedly in favor of Kennedy and the New Frontier was born.

THE TORCH IS PASSED

But I have confidence in our nation, confidence in our economy, and confidence in your ability to meet your obligations fully. I hope that my associates and I can merit your confidence as well. For I can assure you that we love our country, not for what it was, though it has always been great—not for what it is, though of this we are deeply proud—but for what it someday can and, through the efforts of us all, someday will be.

John F. Kennedy, February 13, 1961

The election of John F. Kennedy gave Americans hope. A hope which founded the belief that brighter times lay in the future rather than in the past—that the United States' ultimate greatness had yet to be realized. A belief that each American could and must contribute to this national quest for greatness. A sense that these efforts were not only worthwhile but necessary. A feeling that the United States was entering a period of unprecedented excitement and productivity. A realization that it would take a unified American effort to achieve these lofty but desirable results is what John F.

Kennedy, in his 1037 days as president of the United States communicated to Americans and to the world.

Only with a point of reference can the impact of Kennedy's presence on the nation be seen. In the previous eight years under the Eisenhower administration, the nation experienced a complacency which led to few positive developments in domestic or international affairs. Although the 1950s were prosperous for some, Eisenhower's two terms were plagued by three economic recessions. Socially, Civil Rights came to the forefront and the unrest which characterized the 1960s was born. Eisenhower's indifference to space exploration gave the Soviets and almost insurmountable lead in the space race. Further darkening Eisenhower's tenure, the Cold War continued to chill throughout his first term and hardened during his final four years in office. Socially, the United States was more tame and dull than the previous 30 years. During Eisenhower's administration, a placid, almost stagnant atmosphere gripped the nation.

So when the handsome, intelligent, witty and youthful Kennedy won the 1960 election, he gave Americans hope that the stoical 1950s would yield to an exciting and productive New Frontier. The relatively inexperienced Kennedy used two characteristics to instil hope and expectation in millions of Americans. First, he used his sense of vision and effective communication skills to establish national goals. Second, he wielded a personal charisma rivaled in this century only by the two Roosevelts. The combination of these two strengths gave Americans a national purpose and made them believe that anything was possible.

Vision

No national politician since John Kennedy has displayed such strength of vision. Kennedy had a plan for greatness—a destiny for the United States. However, the young president was more than just eloquent rhetoric; he acquired the necessary funds, persuaded passage of the appropriate legislation and gained the support essential to accomplish the lofty goals he set for himself and for the nation. Kennedy's ideal and unique image of the future focused around resolving three major problems facing the nation: The space race, civil rights and world peace.

After the end of World War II, the Soviets and Americans had been trying to develop rockets which could carry a military payload from one continent to another. In the United States, the thrust of rocket science had been to develop an Intercontinental Ballistic Missile (ICBM) for the military and to virtually ignore the possibilities of making an entry into outer space.

Finally, in 1955 the Department of Defense was directed to proceed with the development of a small satellite. The effort for this project, however, was not to interfere with the ICBM research. Further hampering the space project were budget cuts resulting from the economic recessions. By dividing the rocketry research between the scientific and military communities, the United States hindered its own progress in both projects. The Soviets had combined their scientific and military efforts which earned them a large lead in the space race.

On October 4, 1957 the Soviets won the race to enter space when they launched the Earth's first artificial satellite. With the success of *Sputnik*, the United States' confidence in its superiority in science and technology was dealt a shocking blow. Eisenhower downplayed the significance of *Sputnik* by explaining that the satellite did not directly compromise the security of the United States. However, the president's perception of the significance of *Sputnik* was not shared by all. The popular belief was that the country which was able to harness space first would have a marked military advantage over the other. With the Soviets' perceived advantage, many feared that governments all over the globe might dump the United States as an ally and align themselves with the communist power.

Further tarnishing American pride was the success of *Sputnik II* and the launch failure of a similar satellite two months later by the United States; the Vanguard rocket lifted a few feet off the launching pad and exploded. The complacency fostered by the Eisenhower administration toward science and technology had raised its ugly head.

Less than three months after Kennedy took office the Soviets won the race to put a man in space. This was the last straw for the new president. He was no longer willing to have the United States play second-fiddle to the Soviets. Kennedy asked Vice President Johnson, who he appointed as chairman of the Space Council, to assess the United States' position in the space race. Johnson was to provide answers to the following questions:

1. Do we have a chance of beating the Soviets by putting a laboratory in space, or by a trip around the moon, or by a rocket to go to the moon and back with a man. Is there any other space program which promises dramatic results in which we could win?

2. How much additional would it cost?

3. Are we working twenty-four hours a day on existing programs? If not, why not? If not, will you make recommendations to me as to how work can be speeded up.

4. In building large boosters should we put our emphasis on nuclear, chemical or liquid fuel, or a combination of those three?

5. Are we making maximum effort? Are we achieving necessary results?

The strength and energy conveyed in this private document is less eloquent but testifies to the genuine nature of the vigor so characteristic of Kennedy's public rhetoric. Once he had this information, the president made the decision to put a man on the moon. Kennedy's strength in establishing and communicating a vision transformed the national effort from attempting to keep up with the Soviets to reclaiming scientific and technological superiority for the United States. But rather than simply stating that he wanted to aid the lagging American effort in the space race, Kennedy set a specific national goal in a televised speech on May 25, 1961 to a special session of the Congress:

Now it is time to take longer strides—time for a great American enterprise—time for this nation to take a clearly leading role in space achievement, which in many ways may hold the key to our future on earth.

I believe we possess all the resources and talents necessary. But the facts of the matter are that we have never made the national decisions or marshaled the national resources required for such leadership. We have never specified long-range goals on an urgent time schedule, or managed our resources and our time so as to insure their fulfillment.

. . . I therefore ask the Congress, above and beyond the increases I have earlier requested for space activities, to provide the funds which are needed to meet the following national (goal): . . . I believe that this nation should commit itself to achieving the goal, before this decade is out, of landing a man on the moon and returning him safely to earth. No single space project in this period will be more impressive to mankind, or more important for the long range exploration of space; and none will be so difficult or expensive to accomplish . . . But in a very real sense, it will not be one man going to the moon—it will be an entire nation. For all of us must work to put him there . . .

This vision statement focused the efforts of all parties involved—the Congress, the military, the regulatory agencies, the scientists and the astronauts to a common purpose. A purpose provided the necessary motivation for such a large venture. Because each party could see how its actions fit into the larger picture, it helped to eliminate wasted effort. It also had a dramatic effect on the Congress. Support for his program was overwhelming; there was only minor opposition in the House of Representatives while the Senate debated the issue for only an hour. With $500 million in newly appropriated funds, the space program was on its way to the moon. A concrete plan to produce a successful moon shot was approved in October of 1962.

Because Kennedy was able to mobilize the public, Congress and NASA toward one desirable, common goal, there was little chance it could fail. The decade of long and countless hours of hard work that went into the space program grew into fruition on July 20, 1969. The echoes of Kennedy's vision statement could be heard in Neil Armstrong's immortal words, "That's one small step for a man, one giant leap for mankind."

Kennedy's visionary powers, however, were not confined to the stars. He was also able to aim them down to what was below the bottom of the existing social ladder. As he took office, the nation's treatment of black Americans was shameful. The black race did not enjoy equal voting rights, equal protection under the law, equal access to jobs, equal living conditions or equal opportunity for education to that afforded whites. It was clear that the same liberties and freedoms promised to all American citizens in the Declaration of Independence were not obtainable by black Americans.

The movement to rectify this situation began in 1954 when the Supreme Court overturned the *Brown vs. Board of Education* decision. "Separate but equal" facilities were no longer permissible under the law, and with much conflict and resistance, schools began to integrate in the South. During Eisenhower's administration the first significant civil rights legislation was passed since the Reconstruction period following the Civil War. Eisenhower made the historic decision to send federal troops to Little Rock, Arkansas in 1957 to uphold the *Brown* decision and force the integration of Central High School. Eisenhower viewed the role of the president simply to uphold the Constitution. He thought of integration as a moral rather than political issue, and that it wasn't desirable or possible to legislate morality.

Eisenhower missed the point. Integration and the larger struggle for equal civil rights was, is and must be both a moral and political issue. Any issue which concerns the fundamental freedoms and liberties of millions of Americans, in every city, county and state, must be addressed by the government of the United States. Since Reconstruction, this issue had been a raw nerve ending in the South and talk of reform was pouring salt on the wound. But racial discrimination was not just a product of the South. Indeed, the more overt and obvious defiances of federal civil rights legislation did occur in the South. Many Northern whites were equally guilty of the more subtle forms of discrimination as in housing and job opportunities.

President Kennedy had difficulty passing civil rights legislation because of a strange political coalition that had developed. To form what some termed a third political party, Western conservatives sided with Southerners on many issues including civil rights. A commonality existed between the West, which was predominantly conservative, and the South: both were largely rural and agricultural. This meant that many of the Republican policies were more appealing to Southern Democrats than those of the industrial, urbanite Northern liberals. When the two factions voted together they held a majority in the House and the Senate, but lacked the votes to override a presidential veto. This coalition hindered the efforts of Democratic Presidents Roosevelt, Truman and especially Kennedy. Because he was elected to the White House by a slim margin, he did not have the political clout afforded to landslide presidents.

Another barrier to civil rights legislation was the attitude of the nation in the early 1960s. For over 250 years the black race in America legally was property. Only in the last century did this change—but it was a small change. Black Americans were treated as second-class citizens and were excluded from white culture. Nationally, only a few blacks could achieve more than menial jobs working for whites. Although the master-slave relationship technically was dead, it's deeply ingrained tradition was still alive in the minds of many Americans. Kennedy realized that these emotions could not be expelled overnight. He was aware that civil rights reform would not be effective if it was shoved down peoples' throats. In the same way they were formed, it was going to take a strong, constant but flexible effort over a long period of time to dispel the racist actions and beliefs.

Civil rights was the most important domestic issue Kennedy faced. The political and emotional factors working against racial equality made it the most dangerous. Balancing the dire need for reform and the explosive nature of the situation, Kennedy set the national agenda by communicating his ideal and unique image of the future to a NAACP rally during the campaign of 1960:

> While we point with pride to the strides we have made in fulfilling our forefathers' dream of the equality of man, let us not overlook how far we still have to go. While we point with concern to denials of civil rights in one part of the country, let us not overlook the more subtle but equally vicious forms that are found in the clubs and churches and neighborhoods of the rest of the country.
>
> Our job is to turn the American vision of a society in which no man has to suffer discrimination based on race into a living reality everywhere in our land. And that means we must secure to every American equal access to all parts of our public life—to the voting booth, to the schoolroom, to jobs, to housing, to all public facilities including lunch counters.

In contrast to the space program, the nation was divided by a great chasm on the issue of civil rights. This made passage of necessary laws for the enforcement of racial equality a much more difficult proposition. Because his hands were tied by the Congress, he was unable to repair the damaged governmental net himself. Instead, he opted to employ the executive powers at his disposal to create a fertile climate for civil rights advancement which would ease the burden of the problem on society. A few of Kennedy's executive actions included pressuring to federally employ more qualified blacks; appointing more qualified blacks to high federal positions; morally denouncing segregation; and pressuring civil leaders to denounce racial discrimination.

A major portion of the injustices of the period did not happen because of a lack of federal legislation. Rather, the federal government simply did not possess the resources to litigate the thousands of illegal actions occurring throughout the country. President Kennedy decided to fight this battle on two fronts. On the less visible front, his strategy was to work with and encourage local officials to abide by the existing laws. If this proved ineffective the Civil Rights Division of the Department of Justice began the litigation procedure. This was the responsibility of the United States attorney general, the position which the president entrusted to his brother Bobby. This effective strategy of giving the local governments the opportunity to act first before federal intervention allowed President Kennedy to avoid an adversarial relationship with third party leadership whose support was essential to the success of the movement.

On the other battlefront, John Kennedy used the high visibility inherent to the presidency to effect changes in the attitudes, beliefs and thus, actions of Americans. Kennedy transformed the heated local conflicts into a broader struggle for freedom and justice. Rather than debate the justness of individuals' actions relating to specific events, he spoke of the common motives behind the boycotts and sit-ins. He recognized the past injustices as wrong, but left the past to brother Bobby and the justice department lawyers. The president asked Americans to envision a brighter future in which all citizens of the United States would be afforded equal rights, equal opportunities and equal protection under the law. He believed that retribution for the past was a short-term benefit while national changes in attitudes and beliefs would bear fruit in the future.

This Kennedy brother one-two punch from opposite ends of the problem was effective. Between June 1960 and June 1961, the Civil Rights Division received 665 complaints compared with 162 the previous year. From 1957 to 1960 only five cases had been filed in court by the Civil Rights Division. In the next three years, over 35 cases had been won with scores more in the process. The lawsuits and the publicity they received was, in much the same way the Truman Committee was the watchdog for war mismanagement, responsible for the prevention of further acts of injustice. The broad shift in attitudes and beliefs opened the door for updated and more aggressive legislation.

As the support for his ideas and policies grew, President Kennedy mounted an effort to pass new civil rights legislation. Primarily the efforts of President Kennedy, The Civil Rights Act of 1964, passed in the July following his death, was the only significant piece of civil rights legislation of Kennedy's administration. However, it was a large contribution to the movement and it did attempt to solve a broad scope of problems. The act standardized voting registration requirements; empowered the attorney general to litigate cases aiding the desegregation of public facilities; gave school districts technical assistance, grants and aid in their efforts to desegregate; allowed the attorney general to litigate for school desegregation; directed all federal departments to use their funds in an nondiscriminatory manner; and prevented employment discrimination on the grounds of race, color, religion, sex or national origin.

Following his death, the Congress was highly sympathetic to Kennedy's programs and legislation. President Johnson capitalized on this sentiment and received Congressional approval for the 1964 act and the 1965 Voting Rights Act. Kennedy's success in achieving a more positive national attitude and awareness for the civil rights issue was the key to Johnson's future legislative accomplishments.

Kennedy's visionary powers had a dramatic effect on the third problem: the struggle for world peace. As John F. Kennedy assumed the presidency in January of 1961, the Soviet Union and the United States possessed the destructive power to end all life on the planet. The relationship between the two superpowers had deteriorated after the end of World War II. Events in Berlin, Korea, Formosa and Eastern Europe created the Cold War. Both countries attempted to prove to the world that it stood for peace while the other was the constant aggressor.

An event which gave merit to such claims by the Soviets occurred during Eisenhower's last year as president. In May of 1960 a United States U-2 reconnaissance aircraft was shot down over the Soviet Union. President Eisenhower reported the aircraft was off-course while gathering weather information. However, the real truth became known; the pilot, Gary Powers, survived and confessed to being a spy which proved to be highly embarrassing to the United States. Soviet Premiere Nikita Khrushchev angrily cancelled the planned Paris Summit between the two nations.

Many sceptics believed Kennedy, at a youthful 43 years of age, lacked the maturity and experience to responsibly conduct the delicate U.S.-Soviet relationship. Indeed, foreign affairs would prove to be his greatest challenge, but two of Kennedy's accomplishments demonstrated to the world that the United States, above all, wanted peace. In a campaign speech Kennedy noted that, "In the two areas where peace can be won, in the field of disarmament and in our representations abroad, this country has been ill-served." Kennedy amended this situation with two major accomplishments. First, the president established the Peace Corps which gave youthful idealists, who identified so well with Kennedy, the opportunity to personally make the world a better place. Second, he negotiated a nuclear test ban treaty with Khrushchev and British Prime Minister Harold Macmillan making the Earth a safer place to live. Both acts gave Americans and citizens of the world hope that human life would continue to flourish.

The Peace Corps was not Kennedy's idea. The original idea of a worldwide youth service program had been discussed after World War II. In January of 1960 proposals for a similar program were introduced in the Senate and House but produced little excitement. Kennedy, however, was very interested in the idea. As he campaigned at college campuses that summer and fall, he began to see the potential for such a program using the efforts and energies of American youth. In a major campaign speech in San Francisco on November 2, Kennedy transformed the idea into a campaign promise and another visionary aspect of the New Frontier:

> I . . . propose that a peace corps (be established) of talented young men and women, willing and able to serve their country . . . well qualified through rigorous standards, well trained in the languages, skills and customs they will need to know . . .
>
> This would be a volunteer corps, and volunteers would be sought among not only talented young men and women, but all Americans, of

whatever age, who wished to serve this great Republic and serve the
cause of freedom.

I am convinced that the pool of people in this country of ours
anxious to respond to the public service is greater than it has ever been
in our history. I am convinced that our men and women, dedicated to
freedom, are able to be missionaries, not only for freedom and peace,
but to join in a worldwide struggle against poverty and disease and
ignorance . . . I think this country in the 1960's can start to move
forward again. We can demonstrate what a free society, freely moving
and working, can do.

Because the idea had been floating in the public domain for
15 years there were numerous reports and academic papers
exploring the possibilities of a youth service program. After the
election, Kennedy asked his brother-in-law, Robert Sargent Shriver,
Jr., to sort through the available information and prepare a detailed
report as to how the program could be organized and then to execute
the plans. "Sarge" Shriver was an excellent choice to head the
Peace Corps because he was a gifted leader himself and he
possessed a great desire to make the Peace Corps a functioning
reality.

In early February, to help with the enormous job, Shriver
assembled a task force to help organize, plan and execute a Peace
Corps program. The group had been considering plans which
operated on a relatively small scale. Shriver found what he was
looking for in the report "The Towering Task" by Warren Wiggins.
Shriver quickly shifted gears and guided the group's efforts in
Wiggins' direction. The report argued that a youth service program
would fail on a small scale because the impact to that nation could
not be felt. Only if hundreds of volunteers entered a single country,
could the progress be large enough to make a significant difference.
On February 28, 1961 Shriver submitted a report to the president
which closely resembled Wiggins' idea. To speed the program,
Shriver's report recommended establishing the Peace Corps by
executive order rather than through traditional Congressional

channels. Kennedy wasted no time. The next day, March 1, the Peace Corps was established by Executive Order 10924.

Each volunteer had his or her own personal reasons for joining the Peace Corps, but Brent Ashabranner, who aided the program in Nigeria, explained the constant theme driving the volunteers:

> They wanted to make some kind of contribution to a better world in a personal, individual way. And for many, perhaps most, this motive was connected with their affection for Kennedy and with the things he had said about building a stronger a better America through helping the poor counties of the world.

The Peace Corps achieved great success. In 1961 over 500 volunteers had been placed in nine different countries and several hundred more volunteers were in training. In 1962 the Congress passed the Peace Corps Act which gave it a certain amount of permanency. By 1986, its 25th anniversary, the Peace Corps had placed over 120,000 volunteers.

It's success cannot be judged strictly by numbers. The efforts of the volunteers helped to dispel the image of "The Ugly American." This term refers to the title of a book by Eugene Burdick and William Lederer which described Americans as ignorant and intolerant of other world cultures and judging them by American standards. Indeed, their efforts helped the image of Americans worldwide. With American volunteers in their own backyard, it was more difficult for naysayers abroad to demonstrate that the United States did not care about their human progress.

The Peace Corps is a perfect example of a leader blending a purely idealistic notion and a realistic solution into a unique and effective program. Many individuals, including the thousands of volunteers, are to be credited for the program's triumphs. The fundamental reason for its initial success, however, is that Kennedy tapped the idealistic energy and duty of service of American Youth which had been dormant throughout the Eisenhower years.

The political and emotional climate of the 1960s made more difficult Kennedy's efforts to negotiate an arms agreement with the Soviet Union. The adjectives "commie", "pinko" and "red" were common language of the 1950s. The terms not only were expressing a bitter distaste but concealed a deep underlying fear of communism. In the same way Americans viewed communism as a threat to the American way of life, Russians perceived capitalism as a threat to their communist society.

This mutual distrust was a product of McCarthyism. Although the senator was censured in 1954 and died in 1957, the fear and loathing of communism he had preached were alive and well. Naturally these feelings bred a mistrust of the Soviet Union in Americans. However, the mistrust was not without foundation. The Soviets did not uphold all the agreements they made at the Yalta and Potsdam Conferences during World War II which enraged Americans. The U-2 and Bay of Pigs incidents made trusting Americans a risky policy for the Soviets.

President Kennedy, however, believed that peace could be won. He hinted of his hopes for reaching an accord with the Soviets in his Inaugural Address:

> ... to those nations who would make themselves our adversary, we offer not a pledge but a request: that both sides begin anew the quest for peace, before the dark powers of destruction unleashed by science engulf all humanity in planned or accidental self-destruction.
> So let us begin anew—remembering on both sides that civility is not a sign of weakness, and sincerity is always subject to proof. Let us never negotiate out of fear. But let us never fear to negotiate.

The idea of negotiating a treaty with the Soviets was distasteful to many members of Congress. Because any treaty must be ratified by two-thirds of the Senate, an agreement seemed doubtful. Contributing to this doubt was the disappointment of Geneva. In March of 1962, the Eighteen Nation Disarmament Committee failed to make any progress toward a treaty. As a result, both the Soviet Union and the United States resumed atmospheric nuclear testing.

The efforts of the Peace Corps and the ultimate feeling of relief on the outcome of the Cuban Missile Crisis helped improve the United States' relationship with the Soviets. The Cold War had thawed, be it ever so slightly, but it was an opening for Kennedy. The president took this opportunity to travel the country and explain the benefits of such a treaty. In his commencement address at American University in June of 1963 he expressed his thoughts on Soviet-American relations:

> Both the United States and its allies, and the Soviet Union and its allies, have a mutually deep interest in a just and genuine peace and in halting the arms race. Agreements to this end are in the interests of the Soviet Union as well as ours . . . So, let us not be blind to our differences — but also let us direct attention to our common interests and to the means by which those differences can be resolved. And if we cannot end now our differences, at least we can help make the world a safe place for diversity. For, in the final analysis, our most common link is that we all inhabit this small planet. We all breathe the same air. We all cherish our children's future. And we are all mortal.

This positive and optimistic speech was warmly received in Moscow. Because Kennedy high-lighted Soviet-American commonalties and their importance to such an agreement while downplaying their differences, the speech gave the Soviets hope that an acceptable accord could be reached. In May, a conference was scheduled to begin July 10 in Moscow to discuss a treaty. As Kennedy was preparing his negotiating team, he was careful to get input from Congressional members. President Kennedy incorporated many of their thoughts, opinions and ideas into his strategy.

On August 5, 1963 Secretary of State Dean Rusk signed the document on behalf of the United States. The Treaty of Moscow, as it was referred to, signed by the United States, the United Kingdom and the Soviet Union, prohibited atomic testing in the atmosphere, underwater and in outer space; underground tests were still permitted. However, the agreement would not be valid unless ratified by the Senate. But because the president had consulted the senatorial leadership of both parties before making critical decisions involving the treaty, the Senate felt they had played an active role in establishing the content of the pact. The treaty was ratified on September 22, 1963 by a vote of 80-19.

The Treaty of Moscow was the foundation upon which all future arms agreements would build. It was a symbol that the superpowers could work together to secure peace. The success of the Treaty helped to erode the mutual feeling of mistrust which made possible the warming of the Cold War and the beginning of Detante during the Nixon Administration.

The successes achieved in these three areas—space, civil rights and world peace—testify to the value of a visionary plan for the future. Further testimony to this power resting in a well articulated vision is the lack of an energy policy developed during the 1980s. With the increased awareness and concern for the environment, the extremely popular President Reagan had the opportunity to shift this nation of consumers to an environmentally responsible one. If he had looked to the future and developed a comprehensive policy and communicated where he wanted it to lead there is little doubt that the public would have rallied behind the effort. Without such a visionary statement, or plan of action, the United States is forced to weather the storms of the highly volatile energy market.

Charisma

The second characteristic Kennedy possessed that instilled a sense of hope and excitement in Americans was his unique personal charisma. His charisma came from three sources: his visionary approach to problems, his attractive and youthful image, and his extraordinary sense of humor. These were characteristics with which idealistic young Americans could identify. Kennedy's election was a symbol that youth, vitality and vigor were "in" and stoicism and the status quo were "out." It became obvious that the pro-active approach of his ideas and programs was an exciting and dramatic change from Eisenhower's reactive positions. Kennedy capitalized on the idealism and the energy of youth. Americans at middle age and younger became involved in politics, public service and the issues relating to the world around them because Kennedy aroused their common interest of a greater America. Once he had a loyal following, he put his ideas into action.

However, as was witnessed in the Carter administration, effective leadership takes more than just good ideas. Despite his administration commonly being viewed as a failure, President Carter did have a few good ideas—a Middle East peace treaty, arms limitation and an energy policy. Poor execution and his inability to encourage people to follow him strangled the initial excitement of his administration. This by no means suggests that a leader must have good looks and a sense of humor to be effective, but Kennedy had an abundance of those two characteristics which provided a wake-up call to a slumbering nation.

Kennedy's good looks were not his only attributes which the nation found attractive. The public and the press also found his youth and fresh language very appealing. Kennedy had a rare charm that would brighten even the dreariest of rooms. As he entered the briefing room for press conferences, he took bold and confident strides to the podium. His tall and lean frame was fitted with a sharp, immaculately tailored suit. His clean-cut hair and clean-shaven face reminded the audience of the boy next door. His broad genuine smile revealed his perfect white teeth and his eyes emitted a sparkle and energy which captivated his audience. This dazzling appearance commanded their attention.

Influencing his appearance was John Kennedy's age. At 43 Kennedy was the youngest president elected. Jacqueline was 12 years younger and delivered their second child, John, Jr., just weeks after the election. This youth invading the White House destroyed the fatherly image of the presidency under Eisenhower. Kennedy welcomed this renaissance in his Inaugural Address:

> Let the word go forth from this time and place, to friend and foe
> alike, that the torch has been passed to a new generation of
> Americans—born in this century, tempered by war, disciplined by a
> hard and bitter peace, proud of our ancient heritage--and unwilling to
> witness or permit the slow undoing of those human rights to which
> this nation has always been committed, and to which we are committed
> today at home and around the world.

Kennedy hoped that this new image at the top of government would
trickle down and eradicate the nation's feelings of complacency as
well.

Kennedy's rhetoric is the most enduring symbol of his three
years in the White House. Because his language was a reflection of
his intellect, it was thought provocative—his ideas were not aged
rehashments, they were fresh and challenged Americans to think of
improvement and progress. His call to put a man on the moon
incited Americans to dream of the possibilities of exploring outer
space. His call for an end to racism provoked images of a
harmonious society in which Americans would be judged, as Martin
Luther King, Jr. said, "by the content of their character not by the
color of their skin." His call to public service in the Peace Corps
challenged the idealistic youth to imagine a world without poverty
and disease. His call for a nuclear test ban treaty allowed the world
to think of the day when war would be a thing of the past. Despite
the harsh words of his critics, his accomplishments in these areas
demonstrate that there was substance behind his elegant style.

Kennedy's rhetoric conveyed to America that he had an eye
on the future. He was not so concerned how history would view
him as how it would reflect on how his generation took advantage of
the opportunities the 1960s offered. Kennedy's message was
positive, "we can do better," and he communicated urgency—that
the time for action was now. That if America was to be a greater
nation, it could no longer procrastinate in making it so.

As were his ideas, his rhetoric was fresh and crisp never
clumsy or wordy. It was strong and direct while it was eloquent.
Kennedy employed short, easy to remember phrases to cement his

ideas in the minds of Americans. His historic and visionary, "Ask not what your country can do for you—ask what you can do for your country," made his call for a sense of civic duty memorable. "Let every nation know, whether it wishes us well or ill, that we shall pay and price, bear any burden, meet any hardship, support any friend, oppose any foe, to assure the survival and success of liberty," quickly informed the world of American foreign policy. "Let us never negotiate out of fear. But let us never fear to negotiate," efficiently described his attitude toward arms reduction talks. Because Kennedy was in control and command of the English language, his words and actions guided the United States closer to his vision of a greater America.

Despite his stunning appearance, humor may have made the largest contribution to Kennedy's personal charisma. Charisma is not solely reliant on humor, but frequently those whom we view as being charismatic are blessed with a sense of humor. This was true of John Kennedy. Rarely was his wit slapstick; he was a master at finding (or making) humor in the everyday life of politics and current events. Very apparent in his humor was Kennedy's intellect. President Kennedy was at his witty best in his weekly press conferences because they were a magnificent showcase for his spontaneous wit. The following are some of his best responses where he displayed the Kennedy charm and sarcastic humor.

REPORTER. The Republican National Committee recently adopted a resolution saying you were pretty much of a failure. How do you feel about that?

PRESIDENT KENNEDY. I assume it passed unanimously.

REPORTER. There's a feeling in some quarters, sir, that big business is forcing you to come to terms. Businessmen seem to have the attitude, "Now we have you where we want you."

PRESIDENT KENNEDY. I can't believe I'm where big business wants me.

REPORTER. Mr. President, have you narrowed your search for a new Postmaster General? Are you seeking a man with a business background or a political background?

PRESIDENT KENNEDY. The search is narrowing, but there are other fields that are still to be considered, including even a postal background.

Kennedy was also able to laugh with reporters during his campaign for president:

REPORTER. President Eisenhower has been pretty a pretty popular president. How much of a factor do you expect him to be in the campaign?

SENATOR KENNEDY. Well, I would be glad to have his cooperation but I think he is already committed.

REPORTER. Senator, Governor Brown (California) today issued a very optimistic statement about your chances. Yet the field poll shows Nixon running ahead. Which of these two experts do you believe?

SENATOR KENNEDY. I believe Governor Brown.

Another arena in which Kennedy demonstrated his flair for humor were the Gridiron dinners. Each year legislators, lobbyists, bureaucrats, columnists, editors and publishers gather at Washington's Gridiron Club for an evening of speeches, skits and songs all in off-the-record good humor. No individual or organization, including himself, was safe from Kennedy's sarcasm at these events. At one of the dinners Kennedy joked, "I'm glad to see my old friend Arthur Krock here. Mr. Krock has been at ever major dinner in history—except the Last Supper--and he had a relative at that one."

At the dinner during the 1960 presidential campaign, Kennedy poked fun at fellow candidate Lyndon Johnson:

I had a dream the other night, and I told Stuart Symington and Lyndon Johnson about it in the cloakroom yesterday. I told them how the Lord came into my bedroom, anointed my head, and said, "John Kennedy, I hereby appoint you the President of the United states." Stu Symington said, "That's strange, Jack, because I had a similar dream last night, in which the Lord anointed me and declared me President of the United States." And Lyndon Johnson said, "That's very interesting, gentlemen, because I had a similar dream last night—and I don't remember anointing either one of you."

Kennedy was annoyed with some of the questions asked by Sara McClendon at press conferences. At the time of the dinner, Jacqueline was on a state visit in India. Said Kennedy, "I saw my wife's picture watching a snake charmer in India. As soon as I learn Sara McLendon's favorite tune I'm going to play it."

Kennedy was brilliant with the parody—on this occasion it was his Inaugural Address:

We observe today not a celebration of freedom but a victory of Party, for we have sworn to pay off the same party debt our forebears ran up nearly a year and three months ago, Our deficit will not be paid off in the next hundred days, nor will it be paid off in the first one thousand days, nor in the life of this Administration. Nor perhaps even in our lifetime on this planet. But let us begin.

Kennedy's wit not only endeared him to the public and to the press, but he used it as a weapon to manage sensitive issues. Used properly, humor can diffuse uncomfortable questions that do not answer well with facts figures and reason. An appropriate one-liner can be an effective response to a question that would otherwise require a "no comment." Kennedy normally used his eloquent rhetoric to reflect his sharp intellect as he responded to serious issues—as is necessary for a candidate or politician—but frequently he relied on his great arsenal of wit to manage two awkward questions concerning his 1960 campaign: his wealth and his religion.

Kennedy used humor to divert attention away from the non-issue of wealth so that the focus of his campaign might be his economic programs, his foreign policies or his concerns on domestic affairs. Kennedy met the concern of his father's wealth with humorous remarks:

> The secretary of Commerce has announced a major new plan for restricting the outflow of gold to France—by keeping my father at home this year.

> I just received a telegram from my father. He says, "Don't buy one more vote than you need. I'll be damned if I'll pay for a landslide.

The prospect of Kennedy being the first Catholic president was an alarming issue to many people. It was feared that if Kennedy was elected, that the president would be receiving his orders from the Pope. Again Kennedy used wit where facts and logic would only go so far:

> I sat next to Cardinal Spellman at dinner the other evening, and asked him what I should say when voters questioned me about the doctrine of the Pope's infallibility. "I don't know, Senator," the Cardinal told me. "All I know is that he keeps calling me Spillman."

Kennedy recalled the plight of Al Smith, a Catholic who lost the election of 1928 on the basis of his religion:

> Some circles invented the myth that after Al Smith's defeat in 1928 he sent a one-word telegram to the Pope: "Unpack." After my press conference on the school bill (opposing aid to parochial schools) I received a telegram from the Pope myself: "Start packing!"

There were other, smaller issues in which Kennedy used humor to diffuse the questions. It helped belittle the experience Richard Nixon gained in his Kitchen Debate with Khrushchev: "Mr. Nixon may be very experienced in his kitchen debates. So are a great many other married men I know." Soon after Kennedy took office, there was a public outcry upon his appointment of brother Bobby as United States attorney general. As the chief prosecutor for the United States, Bobby was only 35 years old and had no trial experience. Jack Kennedy disposed of the issue with humor: "I see nothing wrong with giving him a little legal experience before he goes into private practice." Kennedy's "answer" to the call of nepotism left the issue inarguable.

Kennedy's speechwriters played an important role in the success of his humor. Because of time constraints, all presidents must rely heavily on aides and speechwriters for many of their prepared remarks but much of the humor and the style were Kennedy's. He enjoyed both the giving and receiving of jokes and comic lines. Prior to press conferences his aides would generate lists of possible questions and in discussing them with the president often created many comical responses. Most of them were not used because they would not appear "statesmanlike" in print. Kennedy was somewhat fearful that he might slip-up and use one of them in front of the press.

Kennedy's humor seemed to say, "If I don't take the issue as a serious problem, then neither should you." This method turned out to be harmless, but if the issues he laughed off had manifested to cause problems during his administration, then his humor would have done a great disservice by deceiving the public. His wealth and religion never were negative factors in his administration. John Kennedy's humor still gets a laugh three decades later, but it had a great impact on the 1960s by bringing a certain amount of life and excitement to the political arena.

GROWTH OF A LEADER

John F. Kennedy was cool, refined and confident on the campaign trail, but the man who became the nation's ultimate decision maker on January 20, 1961 was grossly inexperienced. He lacked experience in administration, executive politics, and he had never made decisions of the magnitude he would need to make in the upcoming months. This inexperience would surface in April as Kennedy approved the Bay of Pigs invasion. In terms of the lack of communication, misjudgments and absence of common sense, the Cuban disaster rates with the charge of George Armstrong Custer at the Little Bighorn. Unlike Custer, however, Kennedy had the opportunity to learn from his mistakes, and his personality grew from the experience. Gone was a certain naivete and innocence he brought to the White House. Although the Bay of Pigs was terribly embarrassing and quite humbling, it caused Kennedy to make important changes in the structure of his administration. This enabled Kennedy to pull the world back from the brink of nuclear holocaust 18 months later during the Cuban Missile Crisis.

Bay of Pigs

In January of 1959 Fidel Castro successfully completed his guerilla coup overthrowing the Batista regime in Cuba. Although not yet formally a communist, Castro was a Marxist which made the United States suspicious of his movement. Throughout the two-year struggle, support for Batista had eroded and overt American intervention on his behalf would have been a classic example of American imperialism and interference. In a show of good faith, the United States immediately recognized Castro's new government. However, the United States miscalculated the intentions of Castro.

Anti-American sentiments had grown south of the American border because the United States halted much of its aid to Central and South American countries to focus resources on the Cold War. In 1958 Vice President Richard Nixon undertook an eight-nation goodwill tour of the region. He was met with great hostility. His tour was cut short because he was mobbed and pelted with stones and eggs in Peru and Venezuela. Castro communicated Latin America's hostile sentiments in many colorful speeches which were applauded by the Soviets. As Castro snubbed the United States, he wooed the Soviet Union. The situation grew worse for the Eisenhower administration as Castro seized and federalized American property in Cuba. Eisenhower, very concerned with these events, was developing a plan to deal with the problem. This responsibility fell on the Central Intelligence Agency. The strategy was to covertly encourage and aid the anti-Castro movements in Cuba which the CIA predicted would result in a revolution, ousting Castro. The situation further deteriorated and less than a month before Kennedy took office, Eisenhower broke off diplomatic relations with Cuba.

After months of discussion and planning, President Kennedy approved an invasion consisting of 1400 anti-communist Cuban exiles. This "Cuban Brigade" was trained by the CIA in the mountains of Guatemala because the United States did not want to be connected with the operation. After an air strike by Brigade pilots to destroy Castro's air force, the Brigade's mission was to land on the beach of the Bay of Pigs on the southern coast of Cuba, establish a beachhead and declare themselves as a government in opposition to Castro. The logic followed that the anti-Castro sentiment would erupt throughout Cuba and a civil war would ensue. The United States could then overtly support the rebels in their overthrow of the Castro regime. The CIA informed the president that even if they were unsuccessful, the exiles could escape to the mountains and conduct a guerilla war against Castro.

At dawn of April 15, two days before the landing, a small squadron of B-26 aircraft painted with Cuban markings attacked three Cuban air bases. One plane landed in Miami after the raid and the pilot claimed that the raiders were Cubans disenchanted with Castro and had been planning their escape for months. The American press, Castro and the entire world saw through the story. His plane had a metal nose-cone while all of Castro's were made of plastic. His machine gun was found to not have been fired and he was wearing civilian clothes—a white T-shirt, green pants and a baseball cap.

Strategically, it did not make sense for the CIA to plan this raid 48 hours before the landing. It gave Castro a warning that an invasion was imminent, and he placed all of his armed forces on alert. In the early morning of Monday April 17, 1961, the invasion began at the Bay of Pigs. A number of equipment failures and

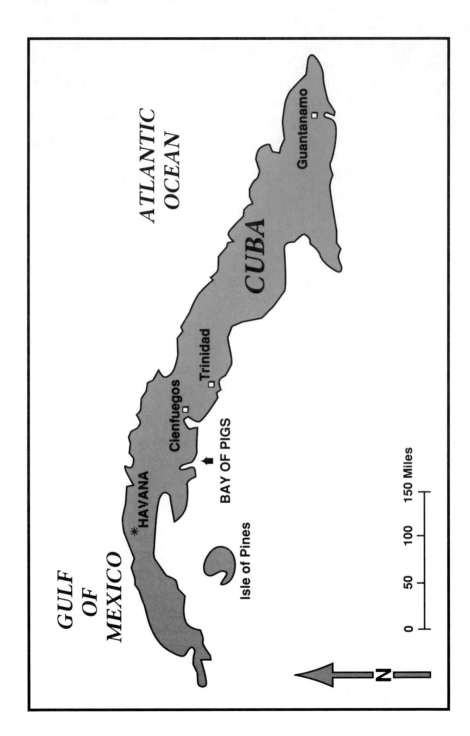

misjudgements due to inaccurate CIA information put the invasion force behind schedule. One of the ships sank on a coral reef the CIA had determined was seaweed. As the troops hit the beach they encountered light resistance, but the gunfire alerted civilians in the area to the operation. Also alerted was a communications center 100 meters from the shore. CIA intelligence reported there would be no communications in the invasion area, but Castro was now aware of the invasion. He instructed his air force commander to destroy the supply ships for if they were able to unload their food and ammunition, the Brigade might be able to sustain the beachhead.

Castro's air force was insignificant compared to the U.S. Naval firepower 20 miles off Cuba's southern shore. However, his few quick jets were vastly superior to the small squadron of slow B-26 targets flown by Brigade and CIA-recruited American pilots. In addition, they could not adjust to the rapidly changing needs of the ground fighters because their base was 600 miles and three hours of flight time away in Nicaragua. On the first day of the invasion Castro's air force shot down nine of these B-26's. Also destroyed were the medical and supply ships in the Bay. The Brigade was being routed and waited for the CIA-promised air support from the U.S. Navy. It never came.

President Kennedy never intended to or perceived a need to commit U.S. armed forces for the operation. Intervention would have given the accurate appearance that the United States had planned the operation. Kennedy was concerned that if he moved on Cuba, it would create an excuse for the Soviets to move on Berlin or other vulnerable parts of the world. Kennedy gave his approval to the plan because his advisors assured him in writing that the operation would succeed without participation by the United States. Given this information, Kennedy declared at a press conference on April 12 that the United States would not interfere in Cuban affairs. Surprisingly, the CIA still promised air support to the Brigade.

Although a number of U.S. planes were launched for reconnaissance from the aircraft carrier *Essex*, they were not allowed to engage the enemy. Many pilots returned to the *Essex* angry and sick after helplessly watching the Cubans cut the Brigade to ribbons.

The massacre was all but over on Tuesday April 18 as Castro's men drove the invaders, who were painfully low on ammunition, back to the sea. The Brigade was prevented from escaping into the mountains because the beach was surrounded by the large Zapata swamp. Unable to advance, escape or to be rescued from the sea, the Brigade members were picked of one-by-one from helicopters. Even Castro himself joined the turkey-shoot from the air. Only a fortunate few of the 1400 men were able to escape to the sea by night and were picked up by the U.S. Navy. In addition to these anti-Castro exiles, Castro was able to eliminate much of his internal opposition. In Gestapo-like fashion, Castro rounded up thousands of Cubans and placed them in temporary jails. Thus, the Bay of Pigs invasion actually strengthened Castro's hold on Cuba.

Complaint and criticism abroad and from within the United States fell on the young president. His critics offered the affair as evidence that Kennedy was too young and immature to occupy the White House. Many nations—even allies—condemned Kennedy's intervention in a sovereign country. The defeat was also a terrible blow to Kennedy's confidence. He was responsible for sending 300 men to their death and 1100 to imprisonment in Castro's jails. This was the low-point of Kennedy's administration—and of his career—he had never experienced a failure of this magnitude. But what made Kennedy a great leader was that, in this dismal shadow of defeat, he was able to learn and grow so that he would never again make a similar mistake.

Why it failed

The Bay of Pigs was doomed to failure at the planning table because the CIA's intelligence reports were badly flawed. The CIA was solely responsible for gathering the necessary information to insure success for the operation. In addition to the coral reef and communication center errors at the landing site, the CIA's lack of accurate information led Kennedy to make poor assumptions as to the possible outcomes of the operation.

The president was informed that a failed invasion would still permit the Brigade to escape to the hills and conduct a guerilla war against Castro. However, they were actually ordered to fall back to the beach if the operation was failing, while only a handful of the Brigade members had been trained to conduct a guerilla war. Thus, the information the CIA provided the president was contrary to the training and orders it gave to the Brigade.

Many members of the Brigade were quite surprised when they were informed by the CIA that the invasion would take place at the Bay of Pigs. Although they were excluded from any of the planning, the Brigade members saw the obvious flaw of choosing the Bay of Pigs as a landing spot. They believed Trinidad or Cienfuegos to be better invasion locations as a city would provide a population to aid and join the rebellion. In fact, the original invasion plan called for the Brigade to land at Trinidad because this site had the advantage of a port and docks where the supplies could have easily been unloaded. The CIA aborted this site because it was concerned that Castro would think this the "obvious" place for such an operation.

A second flaw in the intelligence was the predicted reaction of the Cuban people. Kennedy was led to believe that the plan he was approving, with the aide of the Cuban underground, would result in military desertions and a public uprising against Castro. However, the CIA nor the Brigade had any means to alert the Cuban underground of the invasion without tipping their hand to Castro. The Cuban leader's popularity had also been underestimated by the CIA. Kennedy approved the operation believing that only two outcomes were possible—a revolution ousting Castro or a prolonged guerilla war. Unfortunately, neither was possible because the CIA had not planned for either contingency.

The third bit of flawed intelligence was the related urgency of the situation. Kennedy was informed that it was a now-or-never operation—that very soon Castro would have the military power to defeat such an operation. Castro, however, already had the ability to repel an invasion. The Cuban Air Force, although small and antiquated, proved effective in destroying the Brigade's supplies and in providing a constant threat from the air. Castro's ground units reacted much more efficiently and powerfully that the CIA had anticipated. Thus, without intervention by the United States, the operation was doomed to fail.

Although approving the covert operation was a large risk for the president, there was also risk involved with cancelling the operation. There was the danger that he would appear to have reversed his stance on the importance of Cuba and Latin America which he explained in a campaign speech on October 18, 1960:

> In Cuba the Communists have gained a satellite and established a base for the attempted infiltration and subversion of all Latin America. In Venezuela angry mobs have assaulted the Vice-President of the United States. In Mexico City rioting crowds have protested American policy and castigated America itself. In Panama anti-American demonstrations have imperiled the security of the Panama Canal. In Brazil, the newly elected President felt it necessary to appeal to rising anti-American sentiment in order to win the election. And every report, every broadcast, every newspaper dispatch from the south brings fresh news of unrest, of tension, of misunderstanding.
>
> Today, time is running out for the United States in Latin America. . . It is time now to renew our understanding and begin to act. For although the Cold War will not be won in Latin America, it may very well be lost there.

In addition, members of the Cuban Brigade had been training for months and were extremely anxious to get the chance to liberate their homeland. A cancelled invasion would have infuriated these men and the press would have been the only arena for them to vent these frustrations. They would have explained that an invasion was planned by Eisenhower, was endorsed by the CIA and Joint Chiefs of Staff but this young inexperienced president had cold feet. In both cases Kennedy would have appeared weak.

John Kennedy accepted the blame for the failed mission, "There's an old saying that victory has 100 fathers and defeat is an orphan . . . But, I will say to you . . . I'm the responsible officer of the government—and that is quite obvious." It would be easy, as it would have been for Kennedy, to blame the failure of the Bay of Pigs on the lack of accurate information furnished by the CIA. However, just as it was the president's responsibility to make the decisions, it was his responsibility to ensure that the information he was receiving was accurate. It was difficult for the president to comprehend how these types of failures and errors could have happened. Special Counsel to the President, Ted Sorensen, with the aide of 20-20 hindsight, gave one explanation:

> . . . they arose because of the newness of the President and his administration. He did not fully know the strengths and weaknesses of his various advisors. He did not yet feel he could trust his own instincts against the judgements of recognized experts. He had not yet geared the decision-making process to fulfill his own needs, to isolate the points of no return, to make certain he was fully informed before they passed, and to prevent preshaped alternatives from being presented to him too late to start anew. Nor were his advisors as frank with him, or as free to criticize each other's work, as they would later become.

In this time of despair, Kennedy displayed a resiliency and a toughness characteristic of many strong leaders. He was determined not to allow the entire experience to be a failure; he would learn from it. He established a four member committee very similar in practice to the Truman Committee. Its thrust was not to point fingers, but to determine what went wrong, why and most importantly, how it could be avoided in the future. To this committee, President Kennedy appointed Joint Chief, General Maxwell Taylor; Attorney General, Bobby Kennedy; Chief of Naval Operations, Admiral Arleigh Burke; and CIA Director, Allen Dulles. This investigation and the president's personal reflections of the events and the process precipitated some major changes in his administration as well as in his personality.

Changes

The biggest change in the administration was in the channels through which information was communicated to the president. In the first three months of the New Frontier, there was not a structured channel for Kennedy to receive information. He would get some from one source, a little more from another and more from a third. This meant that each source could not know what information the president had been given. This hit-or-miss process only gave the president a portion of the available information he would need to make the decision. In short, this fragmentary communication process prevented coordination of his administration's many hands. This is where Kennedy's administrative inexperience was exposed and was one of the major reasons the Cuban disaster was possible.

To rectify this situation, for each issue President Kennedy appointed one trusted member of his administration to head a task force. This person would have the responsibility to do all the necessary research and consulting and then give a detailed report to the president. This person was not necessarily the spokesman for the group but always was a competent administrator.

Another change in the administration resulting from the Bay of Pigs was philosophical in nature. The Kennedy administration shifted from a reactive to a pro-active approach to foreign policy issues. Prior to the Bay of Pigs, the administration would concentrate on a crisis as it happened. After the Bay of Pigs, the administration spent its energy trying to prevent a crisis from happening. Kennedy established committees to monitor the situation and the government's activities in sensitive areas of the world, such as Berlin, Laos and Vietnam. This new procedure enabled the committees to be fully knowledgeable of the situation before a crisis occurred. This gave the president the opportunity to prevent a crisis rather than react to one.

There were also personnel changes in the New Frontier. The most noticeable was the replacement of Allen Dulles by John McCone as the Director of the CIA. Dulles left the CIA as it became apparent that his organization was responsible for poor planning and supplying flawed information for the operation.

John Kennedy went through a noticeable personal change as a result of the disaster. He was more thorough in his quest for information on issues, less trusting of the "experts" and relied more on his own assessments and judgements of a situation. Kennedy still depended on his advisors and staff to give him the necessary information to form a perspective, but as a result of the Bay of Pigs, Kennedy asked them more questions to expose all the facts and any contradictions or flaws. Robert Kennedy used Laos as an example of his brother's new approach:

> (the Joint Chiefs) were suggesting we send troops into Laos. I think we would have sent troops into Laos--large numbers of American troops into Laos—if it hadn't been for Cuba. Because everybody was in favor at the time, initially, of sending troops into Laos.
> (the Joint Chiefs of Staff) said, "We'll send troops in." The plan was: Send these men in, we'll get control of this territory, and we'll be in good shape.
> (JFK) said, "Well, first, how will they get in there?"
> Then they rushed around: "They're going to land at these two airports."
> So he said, "How many can land at the airports?"
> "If you have perfect conditions, you can land a thousand men a day."
> So he said, "How many troops of the Communists are in the surrounding area?"
> They said, "We guess three thousand."
> "How long will it take them to bring up four?"
> "They can bring up five or eight thousand, six thousand in four more days."
> So he said, "What's going to happen if on the third day you've landed three thousand—and then they bomb the airport. And then they bring up five or six thousand more! What's going to happen? Or if you land two thousand—and then they bomb the airport?"
> Well the answer was you dropped a bomb on Hanoi--and you start using atomic weapons!

Obviously, the United States did not send troops to Laos.

Because of the Bay of Pigs, John Kennedy became a proficient administrator and experienced valuable personal growth as a leader. He needed these qualities when he confronted the Soviets as they placed atomic missile bases in Cuba in October of 1962.

The Cuban Missile Crisis

The greatest crisis of the Cold War had its roots in the Bay of Pigs. Khrushchev saw an opportunity after Kennedy fumbled the first major action of his presidency. Khrushchev believed that only a weak leader would have allowed the mission to fail and that this same leader would not risk an invasion of Cuba. His logic followed that the Soviet Union could gain a great advantage by supplying Castro with military aid. The Soviet chairman believed that under the guise of "defensive weapons" he could alter the balance of power existing between the two superpowers by positioning nuclear missiles 90 miles away from the southern shore of United States. Khrushchev's logic made sense and his plan might have worked except for one detail—in the 18 months Khrushchev needed to place the missiles in Cuba, John Fitzgerald Kennedy had blossomed into a strong, effective leader.

Included in the Soviet military aid to Castro were surface-to-air missiles (SAMs), which they contended were needed to deter an American invasion of Cuba. In a prepared statement of September 4, President Kennedy declared that the United States would not permit offensive weapons in Cuba and would use "whatever means may be necessary" to prevent it from happening. The United States had been given numerous assurances by Soviet Ambassador Anatoly Dobrynin that there would not be surface-to-surface missiles or any offensive weapons placed in Cuba. The United States discovered evidence to the contrary on the morning of Tuesday, October 16, 1962.

A high altitude U-2 reconnaisance aircraft had taken pictures of the Cuban military activity. The analysis concluded that some of the SAM sites were, in fact, disguises for medium range intercontinental ballistic missile sites.   Once completed, these missiles could destroy any target in Central America and any city east of St. Louis. President Kennedy called a meeting that morning to inform his advisors of these serious events and to have them determine action plans for his consideration.

This group of advisors became the Executive Committee of the National Security Council or "Ex-Comm." The membership included Robert Kennedy; Secretary of State, Dean Rusk; Secretary of Defense, Robert McNamera; CIA Director John McCone; Chairman of the Joint Chiefs, General Maxwell Taylor; and presidential advisors, Ted Sorensen and McGeorge Bundy. Rounding out the membership were many of the undersecretaries and occasionally Vice President Johnson which gave the advisory group over a dozen members. They met daily for the following two weeks to analyze new information from which they formed and discussed many options for the president's consideration.   To encourage free discussion, President Kennedy was absent from many of the meetings. Often a leader's presence will alter advisor's opinions and recommendations to what he or she perceives the leader wants to hear. This groupthink phenomena causes the discussion to be less frank and the recommendations may not accurately reflect the group's true beliefs.

As more information became available, it was decided to keep everything top secret. Kennedy felt it imperative to show strength and resolution here because, in the eyes of Khrushchev, he had shown weakness at the Bay of Pigs. The president wanted to be in control of the situation as much as possible, and alerting the public, press and world of this crisis before he was ready to act would only tip his hand to the Soviets. Merely stating the problem without offering terms for a solution—and a strong one—would have given Khrushchev the opportunity to dictate the solution.

In the late afternoon of Wednesday October 17, President Kennedy met with Soviet Foreign Minister Andrei Gromyko—an engagement scheduled long before the missiles had been discovered. With the new and rapidly developing events Kennedy was inclined to cancel the meeting but he felt that it might look suspicious. He was also somewhat curious of what the Soviets would have to say. Kennedy was shocked to say the least. Gromyko emphasized that his country would never furnish Cuba with offensive weapons. He stressed that the bulk of the Soviet aid was agricultural to prevent hunger and starvation. He assured the president that the only military aid supplied to Cuba was a few specialists to train the Cubans to operate the purely defensive weapons. Gromyko concluded the session with the assertion that none of the Soviet's aid or weapons could threaten the United States. Later, Robert Kennedy discussed this meeting with his brother, and with his own brand of Kennedy wit, paraphrased the president's reaction to the Soviets' obvious attempt at deception, "The President of the United States, it can be said, was displeased with the spokesman of the Soviet Union . . . "

Further photographs and analysis concluded that there were between 16 and 32 missiles in existence which would be operational within a week. The Ex-comm presented President Kennedy with two options: A "surgical air strike" to destroy the missile sites or a blockade of Cuba to prevent further infiltration of Soviet military supplies into the island nation.

Unlike Kennedy's advisors for the Bay of Pigs, the Ex-comm was divided as to which plan to recommend. The blockade would be performed by the U.S. Navy at a to-be-determined distance from the island. All ships confronting the blockade would be boarded and searched and any ship carrying military supplies would not be permitted to continue. The advisors favoring a blockade argued that it was a first step. They believed that a blockade, although it was a show of strength, was limited pressure which could be modified as the situation changed. Blockade supporters explained that it was a show of force that Khrushchev would understand and respect, yet leave Kennedy in control of the situation. They also reported that, in the view of the Joint Chiefs of staff, an air strike was impractical and that it would lead to an invasion at a cost of thousands of lives.

The air strike plans called for 500 sorties to destroy all military targets in the vicinity of the missile sites. Proponents of the plan claimed that a blockade would fail to remove the missiles and would allow work to continue on existing sites. In this way, they argued, the blockage was closing the door after the horse left the barn. They also pointed out that a blockade would invite a similar action by the Soviets in Berlin.

The following day the Ex-comm gave their recommendations to the president with a slight majority favoring a blockade. After proponents of each option presented their course of action, Kennedy, as he had not done adequately enough with the Bay of Pigs, began asking questions. The resulting discussion caused many advisors to change their opinions. President Kennedy, unsatisfied with the lack of resolution within the group, sensed they had not had enough time to thoroughly explore the options. He asked them to discuss them further the next day and to begin working on the specifics for each option.

The methodology the group used to develop a detailed action plan was remarkably different from that used to plan the Bay of Pigs invasion. The Ex-comm split into two groups: those favoring an air strike and those advocating a blockade. Each group wrote a set of recommendations including an outline for a presidential address to the nation, a message to the allies, a list of predicted Soviet reactions and plans of how to deal with them. The groups then exchanged papers and criticized the plans. The papers were returned and modified to incorporate the critics' suggestions and questions. The committee repeated this process all day Friday and well into the night, but eventually each group produced a comprehensive and thorough plan.

Time was running out and Kennedy had to make a decision. It was a difficult position for Kennedy and the United States. Khrushchev and the Soviets were no longer just testing Kennedy's will. This was a direct attempt to change the balance of power between the two nations, and the longer Kennedy waited, the closer the sites were to being operational.

On Saturday afternoon recommendations for each option were presented to the president at a formal meeting of the National Security Council. After a lengthy discussion and many questions and answers, John Kennedy decided to implement a blockade. He decided against the air strike and invasion for three reasons: it would be viewed as an aggressive act by a large country against a small peaceful one; an air strike would kill hundreds of Soviet personnel at the sites leaving Khrushchev no choice but to retaliate; and the Joint Chiefs agreed that an air strike would not be able to destroy all of the missiles. With the decision made, Kennedy's speech to the nation was scheduled for Monday evening.

Sunday and Monday were spent preparing the speech, deploying the military and informing allies of the serious situation. By Monday afternoon the only remaining task was to inform Congress. His decision was met with criticism. Many Congressional leaders were adamant that Kennedy act with more strength than a blockade would convey. Congress was critical and skeptical but ultimately supported the president. Kennedy was somewhat disturbed after this meeting but believed that had his Congressional critics experienced the five-day deliberations of the Ex-comm, they too, would have favored a blockade.

At 7 p.m. on Monday, October 22, 1962, President Kennedy described the situation and explained his course of action to a national television audience. Kennedy illustrated to the world how the Soviets were the aggressor and requested Khrushchev to reassess his country's position:

> I call on Chairman Khrushchev to halt and eliminate this clandestine, reckless, and provocative threat to world peace and to stable relations between our two nations. I call on him further to abandon this course of world domination and to join in an historic effort to end the perilous arms race and transform the history of man. He has an opportunity to move the world back from the abyss of destruction—by returning to his Government's own words that it had no need to station missiles outside its own territory, and withdrawing those weapons from Cuba—by refraining from any action which will widen or deepen the present crisis—and then by participating in a search for peaceful permanent solutions.

As with the majority of his speeches, Kennedy concluded his remarks with a visionary appeal to the American people:

> The path we have chosen for the present is full of hazards, as all paths are; but it is the one most consistent with our character and courage as a nation and our commitments around the world. The cost of freedom is always high—but Americans have always paid it. And one path we shall never choose, and that is the path of surrender or submission.
>
> Our goal is not the victory of might but the vindication of right— not peace at the expense of freedom, but both peace and freedom, here in this Hemisphere and, we hope, around the world.

At the request of President Kennedy, the following morning, the Organization of American States, (OAS) met to consider the question of a blockade. Without its support, such action by the United States would likely have been ruled illegal by the United Nations and the United States would appear as the aggressor. Because of the previous anti-American sentiments, the Ex-comm was somewhat pessimistic about the outcome of this meeting but to their surprise, the United States not only received unanimous support, but many nations even pledged troops and ships for the cause.

With international law now in his corner, John Kennedy authorized the blockade to take effect at 10 a.m. on Wednesday, October 23. Originally the blockade radius was to be 800 miles from Cuba, but upon suggestion of the committee, President Kennedy moved the intercept line to 500 miles. This was an extremely important decision as it would give Khrushchev additional time to consider his options before the confrontation in the Atlantic. Kennedy realized that it was the worst possible time for a national leader to be forced into a snap decision.

As the Ex-comm met that morning it was calculated that the first Soviet ship would reach the blockade before noon. Robert Kennedy explained the tenseness of the situation:

> The Russian ships were proceeding, they were nearing the five-hundred-mile barrier, and we had to either intercept them or announce we were withdrawing. I sat across the table from the President. This was the moment we had prepared for, which we hoped would never come. The danger and concern that we all felt hung like a cloud over us all and particularly over the President.

The world held its breath. One small mistake by either side could rapidly escalate the situation into a military exchange resulting in a brief nuclear war killing all human life. At 10:30 a.m. the committee received a message that the Soviet ships were stopping dead in the water and some were even turning back. Kennedy immediately gave orders not to interfere. It was a reprieve. Both Kennedy and Khrushchev now had more time to consider their options.

On Thursday Kennedy sent another message to Khrushchev asking him to consider that the root of this crisis was the fact that the Soviet Union had deliberately and repeatedly deceived the United States in their interests in Cuba. Kennedy informed his Soviet counterpart that the only way to resolve this dangerous situation would be for the Soviet Union to remove their missiles from Cuba. Later that day a passenger ship was allowed to pass the blockade. Because there was so much that could potentially go wrong Kennedy did not risk boarding and searching a ship with 1500 passengers. However, he was painfully aware that at least one ship would need to be boarded and searched to demonstrate his resolution to Khrushchev.

This first search would occur the next morning. Kennedy personally selected the Panamanian-owned ship *Marucla* to be the first ship to be boarded. This would convey his determination but since the ship was not owned by the Soviets, it did not directly provoke a Soviet response.

On Friday, ABC News State Department correspondent John Scali received a phone call from Alexander Fomin, a counselor at the Soviet embassy asking him to meet for lunch immediately. Over lunch, Fomin, a close friend of Khrushchev, asked Scali to deliver a message to the State Department. It was a proposed solution to the crisis where the Soviet Union would remove its missiles if the United States would end the blockade and give assurances that it would not invade Cuba.

Scali returned to his office at the State Department at 4 p.m., typed a memorandum of his meeting and relayed it to the State Department intelligence chief. This information was quickly relayed to the Ex-comm and President Kennedy. Simultaneously the American Embassy in Moscow began sending a long message from Khrushchev to Kennedy. Because of its length the translation and transmission took over three hours.

This emotional letter from Chairman Khrushchev explained that the Soviets did not want a third world war and that steps needed to be taken to avert the death and destruction such a war would cause. The Soviet chairman informed Kennedy that no missiles could be found on any of the ships because they were already in Cuba. Khrushchev proposed a solution very similar to the one explained to Scali by Fomin. Kennedy went to bed much more optimistic that the crisis could be solved without war.

The optimism of the previous night was snuffed-out on Saturday morning. Another letter had been received from Khrushchev. This one was cold and very formal while proposing that the Soviet Union would remove its missiles from Cuba in exchange for the United States removing its missiles from Turkey. Kennedy had ordered these sites to be removed once in the Spring of 1962 and once later in the summer. The Turkish government had requested the United States leave them as the military bases were a source of income for the nation. Kennedy was very displeased upon discovering that his orders had not been followed. If there was any optimism remaining, it was gone after the Ex-comm received its next piece of information. A U-2 aircraft had been shot down while taking pictures of the missile sites killing the pilot, Major Rudolph Anderson, Jr.

This greatly changed the situation. The president could not maintain the reconnaisance flights without protecting his pilots. This would require bombing the SAM sites in Cuba. Such a situation Kennedy had hoped to avoid because once the shooting started, a nuclear war might have been the only way to stop it. The president, despite the advice of the Ex-comm, decided not to attack the missile sites. To give diplomacy one last chance, he reviewed the prepared responses to Khrushchev's second letter. Robert Kennedy and Ted Sorensen suggested an alternate solution. They advised the president to ignore Khrushchev's second letter and to respond to his first proposal.

President Kennedy informed the Soviet Chairman that he would accept the terms of his first letter but emphasized that the first step would be the withdrawal of missiles from Cuba. It worked. The following morning, President Kennedy was informed by Khrushchev that the Soviet Union was removing the missile sites in Cuba and that the work could be inspected by the United Nations. The blockade was ceased and the crisis, for all practical purposes, was over.

Kennedy was successful in meeting this Soviet challenge in the Cuban Missile Crisis for two reasons: he did not execute the first and obvious option presented to him and he used foresight to predict Khrushchev's response to his actions.

Most of Kennedy's advisors and Congress believed the United States' response should have been an air strike and an invasion of Cuba. This was also Kennedy's initial feeling but he realized that he did not have all the facts and believed that such a major decision required more thought. Many of Kennedy's critics claim that a strong leader would have cited the Monroe Doctrine as legal grounds and authorized the invasion. This course of action would have been that of a foolish leader—we can only hope that in the future all men and women placed in a role of such responsibility would exhaust all other options before plunging the world into a rapidly escalating chain of events which could culminate in nuclear war.

Because President Kennedy was very careful to consider the consequences of his actions, his efforts averted a military conflict while maintaining the military status quo. His decision making process failed during the Bay of Pigs because he lacked the necessary information to form and accurate perspective of the situation. The eighteen months since that incident provided the time for him to remove those bugs from his system.

*   *   *

President John F. Kennedy taught the nation and the world at least three important lessons in his 1037 days in the Oval Office. First, he proved that by communicating a strong vision that even placing a man on the moon was not too far out of reach. Second, his humor showed that no matter how responsible the position a person occupies, it is possible, if not necessary, to have a sense of humor. And finally, he demonstrated the wisdom and necessity to learn from mistakes.

The new feelings of hope and civic responsibility Kennedy fostered in Americans died with him in Dallas in November of 1963. Lyndon Johnson exuded a different feeling to Americans. His war on poverty could be viewed as a positive step along the path Kennedy envisioned years earlier, but Johnson's other war—Vietnam—evoked the feelings of anger, mistrust and frustration in many Americans who had been so moved by the passing of the torch.

Chapter 4

Lee Iacocca

Lido (Lee) Anthony Iacocca is one of the best examples of
an American blessed with a highly efficient management style and a
highly effective leadership ability. While Susan Anthony, Harry
Truman and John Kennedy all were much more leaders than they
were managers, Iacocca possessed and exhibited the necessary
balance between management and leadership to succeed in the
business world. The other three leaders (and King in the following
chapter) were involved with social and political change while
Iacocca was advancing through business. Because of inherent
differences within the systems, Iacocca would be the first to explain
that success in one field does not translate to success in another.
There are, however, common characteristics that highly efficient and
effective people in both politics and business share. Iacocca's
decisiveness and resiliency made him efficient; his vision made him
effective and established him as a true leader in the business
community.

Lee Iacocca, born October 15, 1924, was the second child of
Italian immigrants in Allentown, Pennsylvania. His father, Nicola,
was a great entrepreneur; he started business in America by opening
a hot dog restaurant. He soon diversified and opened a movie
theater and one of the nation's first car rental agencies. Cars were
Nicola's passion—he loved to tinker with his Model-T Ford and he
was always trying to improve the design. This influence, in
conjunction with that of a family friend who owned a Ford
dealership, was responsible for Lee's desire to work in the
automobile business.

Lee was always at the top of his class, but grade school
introduced him to the pains of racism. Most Allentown residents
were Pennsylvania Dutch, and his Italian name and heritage made

him an outsider. Lee would occasionally get into fights with his prejudiced classmates as they frequently slurred his nationality. As he grew older he developed into a good public speaker and joined the school's debate team. From that point he rarely participated in fist-fights—he would talk to the aggressor and avoid violence.

At age 15 Iacocca caught rheumatic fever and spent six months in bed where he developed an interest in reading. The illness prevented him from participating in sports and upon his recovery he devoted his time to the debate team and the drama club. He was an avid music enthusiast and spent his weekends listening and dancing to the big-band era jazz.

The United States entered WWII after the Japanese bombed Pearl Harbor during his senior year of high school. Iacocca wanted to join the Army Air Corps (predecessor of the Air Force) but the army would not accept him because of his bout with rheumatic fever. Disappointed, Iacocca enrolled at Lehigh University to become an engineer. He was fortunate to attend college at that point in history; most college-age men had been drafted which meant that Iacocca's classes were small and personal. As a result, he received an excellent education. While at Lehigh, he reported for the school paper and eventually was promoted to layout editor. His goal upon graduation was to work for the Ford Motor Company. Because his grades were excellent and he was impressive in the interviews, Ford offered him one of the 50 slots in their annual training program. However, another option opened for Iacocca; he was awarded the Wallace Memorial Fellowship at Princeton University which gave him the opportunity to further his studies. Iacocca visited the campus and immediately decided to earn a masters degree before entering the workforce.

After completing his post-graduate degree in 1946, Iacocca began work as an engineer trainee at Ford, but he quickly realized that engineering was not what he wanted to do. He wanted to be where the action was—sales and marketing. Ford, however, hired him as an engineer and emphasized that if he wanted to work in another area, he would have to find the job on his own. He finally found a desk job in the Chester, Pennsylvania district sales office.

Awkward at first, Iacocca became a proficient phone salesman and within two years was promoted to train dealers in the latest sales techniques.

An important benefit of his job in Chester was his association with Charlie Beecham. Beecham was Ford's East Coast regional manager and had a great influence on the young Iacocca. Beecham ingrained in his salesmen the necessity to both take responsibility for and learn from your mistakes. Under his tutelage, Iacocca blossomed and was soon promoted to train Ford salesmen all over the East Coast. Additionally, he met his future wife, Mary McCleary, who was a receptionist in the office.

By 1953 Iacocca became assistant sales manager of the Philadelphia district. In that position he weathered a recession and the resulting Ford reorganization. In 1956 Ford decided to stress safety as opposed to performance in their cars. Unfortunately, the consumers did not respond and sales plummeted. Iacocca's district had the worst selling record in the nation. To deal with this embarrassment, he created his ingenious "56 for '56" plan. His idea was to allow the customer to make payments of $56 a month on a new car after making a 20 percent down payment. Within three months his district was first in the nation, and Ford decided to use his idea as the company's slogan. As a result, Iacocca was promoted to the national truck marketing manager position at the head office in Dearborn, Michigan. During this time, his relationship with Mary McCleary became serious and the two were married in September of 1956.

By early 1960, Iacocca was the Ford division car and truck marketing manager, and in November of that year he was promoted to general manager of the entire Ford division. Iacocca's quick rise through the ranks at Ford was due to his efficient management style and a talent for sales and marketing. His background as an engineer was also very helpful because he could quickly understand and explain the how's and why's of intricate car designs mechanical systems.

In the early 1960s he had the unique opportunity to incorporate vision into his management style and thus elevate himself to the role of a leader. Largely Iacocca's creation, the Mustang broke all industry sales records and demonstrated his talent as a product man. By 1970 he was named president of Ford Motor Company, where he steered the organization to great profitability. A rift developed, however, between Iacocca and the boss—Henry Ford II—the company's chairman. In 1978 he was fired at Ford, but was quickly hired by the ailing Chrysler Corporation as president and CEO. Under Iacocca's management and leadership Chrysler averted bankruptcy and within five years grew into a strong, healthy and profitable company.

Three important periods in Iacocca's career illustrate his unique management-leadership balance: the Mustang project, his firing from Ford and his revival of Chrysler. His decisiveness, resiliency and vision not only revolutionized the automotive industry and saved hundreds of thousands of jobs, but it established him as one of this century's greatest leaders.

THE FORD YEARS

Managers are people who do things right. Leaders are people who do the right thing.

Warren Bennis and Burt Nanus

In 1960 Lee Iacocca was promoted to be the General Manager of the Ford Division of the Ford Motor Company. At only 36 years of age he leaped above many older Ford executives who believed they were in line for the job. This placed a certain amount of pressure on Iacocca as undoubtedly a number of his elder subordinates viewed him with skepticism. But Iacocca was determined to prove his talents to his subordinates, superiors and to the automotive industry. He could not have succeeded in this mighty endeavor without displaying leadership.

The Mustang

To his upper-management position, Lee Iacocca not only brought an efficient management style, but he demonstrated effective leadership. His success was due to a unique blend of two important leadership characteristics: vision and decisiveness. His vision was to create a revolutionary product that would have mass appeal and reestablish Ford as an innovator and a leader in the automobile business. In the Mustang, he was able to create what many car buyers found to be a unique and ideal automobile. In his effort to realize this vision, Iacocca's decisiveness was, in many ways, similar to that of President Harry Truman as he rebuilt Europe and checked communist aggression in Korea.

Both Iacocca and Truman used the three stages of the decision making process: perspective, foresight and execution. Although each molded the process to fit his individual style and circumstances, both used it to implement a program. Truman was decisive in establishing the limited war concept in Korea and rebuilding Europe at Potsdam and through the Marshall Plan. Iacocca's decisiveness was evident as he nurtured and guided the Mustang project from idea to production. Both Iacocca and Truman were operating in competitive and highly stressful atmospheres. Truman was immerse in a rapidly changing contest with the Soviet Union as the fate of the free world hung in the balance. Iacocca had to meet the challenge of General Motors while maintain superiority over number three Chrysler. Both leaders had an excellent knowledge and understanding of the history concerning their respective situations. Time was not an ally for either which necessitated quick—and correct—action.

The early 1960s was a time of great hope and excitement. John Kennedy represented a new generation of Americans in the White House and the economy was improving. The space race was well under way and thousands of Americans were joining the Peace Corps. Ford had enjoyed recent success with the introduction of the Falcon. In the year following its release, the economical compact car sold an automotive record 417,000 cars. General Motors had also introduced a successful product: the Corvair Monza. Both companies had enjoyed profitable years and they were competing in what would be their last decade free of stiff competition from Japan and Europe. These were the conditions under which Iacocca began work on what would be a truly revolutionary automobile.

Upon assuming the top position at the Ford division, he quickly assembled a group of young executives that shared his enthusiasm, confidence, desire and vision. This group met one evening a week at the Fairlane Inn in Dearborn, Michigan to discuss plans, designs and marketing concepts for their "dream" car. Iacocca chaired this "Fairlane Committee" which was comprised of seven members representing engineering, public relations, marketing and production. Iacocca geared the committee to facilitate the three stages of the decision making process.

To form their perspective of the situation they poured over the available market research. They found that the baby boomers were reaching the car-buying age and this huge influx of youth would drastically affect the automobile industry. In addition, the market was becoming more educated as thousands of WWII veterans used the GI Bill to further their studies. Because their research showed that people with more education bought more cars, the Fairlane Committee was able to target yet another demographic group. Research also indicated that two-car families were on the rise and that the market was shifting away from economy cars. Ford was still smarting from the dismal failure of the Edsel in 1957. The consensus was that the Edsel was a car built without a market in mind and that it was tailored to a market that did not exist. Iacocca and his committee were determined not to make the same mistake. In contrast to the Edsel situation, research was telling them that this large and youthful market of the early 1960s was poised and ready to buy the car they wanted to build. After sorting through this vast amount of information, the group was able to form a solid perspective of the situation. They focused on three features key to the success of their product (which still was without a design or even a name): it would have to be stylish, a strong performer and low priced.

With this firm grasp of the situation the committee began using foresight to further shape their project. They avoided designing it as a two-seat model because research showed that they could only hope to sell 100,000 cars; to appeal to a mass market it would have to accommodate a family of four. To obtain the sporty performance they desired, the car would have to be light—they limited the final weight to 2500 pounds. To have a broad appeal, they would have to make the car affordable—they limited the base price to $2500. They wanted a car that would be versatile enough to drive to work, to the club, to church and to the drag strip. Because this large market was so diverse, the committee believed that many options should be made available. The basic car included bucket seats, wheel covers, vinyl trim and carpeting but the buyer could customize his automobile with over fifty options available. This provided the opportunity to make the car as luxurious, economical or sporty as desired. At that time to design and build an new car from scratch would have cost hundreds of millions of dollars. Because Ford was already attempting to cut costs, Iacocca realized that he would have to use many of the basic parts of existing Ford cars. Much of these came from the Falcon which cut the development costs of the Mustang to $75 million. The committee's foresight solved many potential problems before they had a chance to surface. This stage also served to answer many questions of Iacocca's superiors whose approval Iacocca required before beginning production. Ford management was excited by the project and only two superiors voiced opposition to Iacocca's plan. It is important to note that Iacocca was not the person in charge but he had a vision and was able to effectively communicate it to the "bosses." This illustrates that a person does not have to be the boss or the final decision maker to be both visionary and a leader. With approval in the summer of 1962, the Mustang advanced to the execution stage of the process.

Marketing was the major component of the execution phase. The committee decided to unveil the Mustang at the 1964 World's Fair in New York. The industry norm is to introduce cars for any given year the previous fall. Iacocca believed the April date of the event would be a dramatic break from this standard. However, before they could execute the marketing they had other details to decide upon. The April date also meant that they had less than 21 months to finalize the design, work out the production logistics and determine a name for the car. Twenty-one months may appear to be ample time, but to insure a quality product in the automobile business new cars are planned three to five years in advance.

Before any other work could begin on the project, a design had to be agreed upon. In an unprecedented move, Iacocca arranged for a competition among the three Ford design teams. After two weeks of around-the-clock work, Iacocca had seven models from which to choose. In August of 1962 the Mustang was born. Once the design was finalized, all the other production and engineering details fell into place. The Mustang was originally named after the WWII fighter plane, but to create a distinctive image it was quickly associated with the American wild horse. The time frame in which the Mustang was developed was shorter than most other cars produced at Ford or any other major car company. Besides dumb luck, the only way for a quality product to be conceived, designed and produced under these conditions was to have strong, decisive and effective leadership at the helm.

The World's Fair introduction was only part of the brilliant and dramatic marketing of the Mustang. One hundred members of the press were invited to take part in a "Mustang Rally" from New York to Ford headquarters in Dearborn. This allowed the journalists to experience first-hand the quality and uniqueness of the new car. The resulting articles in major magazines and newspapers created a great excitement among not only car buyers but the entire nation as well. For the April 17 introduction date, every Ford dealer in America was delivered at least one Mustang so the public would have the opportunity to personally view the car. This excitement was responsible for the overwhelming response—an estimated four million people visited Ford showrooms in the first weekend.

It soon became apparent that the committee's estimate of selling 100,000 cars in the first year would be low. Demand was so great for the car that Ford opened two additional plants to produce

Mustangs. The options were also selling at record numbers; buyers were spending an average of $1000 on options on a $2500 car! Outpacing even the record-breaking Falcon, the Mustang sold an amazing 418,00 cars in its first year. Profits for the Mustang were an incredible $1.1 billion—in 1964 dollars!

The success of the Mustang was due to Iacocca's leadership and his direction of the thorough research, thoughtful planning and flawless execution—the three stages of the decision making process. This enabled him and the committee to keep the vision firmly in mind as they decisively labored over the multitude of details. The triumph earned Iacocca both a large promotion and the honorable title, "father of the Mustang."

Terminated

Iacocca followed the Mustang with the successful Mark III and Fiesta products. He had proven himself as an excellent product man, demonstrated efficient and decisive management skills and established himself as a leader in the automotive industry. On December 10, 1970, at age 46, his lifelong dream was fulfilled—he was named the president of the Ford Motor Company. He would improve his already sparkling image as an auto executive in his eight years as president. He increased revenues and reduced expenses to earn Ford a $3.5 billion profit during 1977-78. His success would be tempered somewhat by the often petty and childish actions of his boss—Henry Ford II. It was common knowledge in the automobile business that Ford II was prone to arbitrary and ruthless use of his power as "king" of the company. Indeed, Ford II operated his company like a dictatorship and frequently reminded those who differed with his opinion that it was his name on the building. Until the mid-seventies Iacocca and Ford II worked well together, but a rift developed between the two and the resulting two-year conflict was a great test of Iacocca's toughness. Ford II accused, humiliated and slowly stripped him of his power, but Iacocca endured it, showing an admirable resiliency.

His display of resiliency and strength of character did not have an effect on the nation in the same way as Susan B. Anthony's, but like hers, his is an excellent model to study. Another important difference between these two great leaders was that Anthony was challenging broad societal norms and the male-dominated establishment while Iacocca's challenge came from just one person—his boss. Perhaps this is why we may be able to better identify with Iacocca's plight. Because Iacocca's conflict lasted only three years, we can better appreciate the magnitude of Anthony's 50-year commitment to a cause she deeply believed in. Their important similarity is that neither quit as the situation became uncomfortable—the resistance each encountered only deepened their inner resolve and strengthened their determination.

Perhaps the biggest reason for the Iacocca-Ford II conflict was Henry's paranoia. In behavior consistent with that of a dictator, he was constantly worried that someone—anyone—might be trying to challenge his authority. Iacocca was popular with the Ford management, and because of his profitable Mustang, Mark III and Fiesta, the dealers treated him as a revered hero. Ford II viewed this as a danger to his authority. Ford II also wanted his son, Edsel (after whom the car was named) to carry-on the family tradition as the company's chairman, and he viewed the popular and competent Iacocca as a threat to his plans of nepotism. These thoughts and feelings gradually accumulated in Ford II but he never voiced or acted on them until 1975.

In July of that year, Ford II called a meeting of the company's top 500 managers. Without giving advance notice or warning to Iacocca as to the nature of the gathering, he lashed out in criticism of management—of which Iacocca was the top manager. While asserting his authority as "captain of the ship", Ford II maintained that management was not effectively addressing the company's problems. Although he did not mention Iacocca by name, it was very apparent as to who he was displeased with. While this public criticism of an employee contradicts the most basic management principles, it did have a very predictable affect on management: uncertainty, confusion and caution. As a result, employees were more concerned with finding out exactly what the boss meant and not making mistakes, rather than directing their efforts to improve the company.

Things actually became worse for Iacocca and his group of loyal colleagues. Ford II launched an extensive covert investigation of Iacocca's personal and business life. Ford II appointed a special prosecutor who conducted more than 50 interviews of employees of both Ford and its suppliers. Iacocca's friends and associates were put through the wringer in an effort to dredge up filth on Iacocca. Ford executives were living and working in constant fear because many believed their phones and offices to be tapped. This had a dramatic and predictable negative affect on morale. Because Iacocca had operated with high integrity both personally and professionally, the two year, $2 million Ford II probe uncovered nothing.

Instead of offering an explanation or apology, Ford II further humiliated Iacocca by giving him a demotion. In early 1977, Ford II hired a management consulting firm to study the company's structure. The recommendations of this extensive study, which took months and cost millions, was that a three member office be established to replace the existing chairman-president structure. To make the humiliation complete, Ford II installed Phil Caldwell, a former vice president under Iacocca, as the third member of this new office. Ford II mandated that Caldwell would succeed him in the event of death or injury. Summarily, Iacocca was demoted from Ford's number two position to number three. Publicly Iacocca defended the decision but it was having adverse affects on his mental health. Iacocca's private complaints were not only ignored by Ford II, but within a few months a fourth member—Henry's brother, Bill—was added to the office. Although Ford was enjoying enormous profits under his direction, Iacocca was demoted to number four. Despite the frustration and humiliation Iacocca would not quit.

Meanwhile, Ford II had been maliciously firing Iacocca's loyal friends and colleagues in an effort to further inflict pain on the president who refused to resign. However, Ford II did not fire these employees himself; he ordered Iacocca to do the dirty work and fire his friends himself. Ford II mandated that Iacocca fire even Hal Sperlich who had been Iacocca's right hand man on the Mustang, Mark III and Fiesta projects.

Ford II finally made the decision to fire Iacocca, but he announced it in an unprofessional and discourteous manner. The news was leaked to the publisher of the *Automotive News* who called Iacocca late one evening asking if the report was true. Although Iacocca had not been informed of the decision, the previous three years of investigation, demotion and humiliation left no doubt that the rumor was based in fact. The following afternoon Iacocca was summoned to Ford II's office where Henry told him that things just hadn't worked out. Failing to give a specific reason, Ford II fired Iacocca effective October 15, 1978—Iacocca's 54th birthday.

Many have questioned Iacocca's rationale for staying with Ford and not resigning in light of the conflict and resulting humiliations. In his autobiography, he explained that he believed justice would prevail—that the Ford board of directors would back the popular and competent president. Unfortunately (or fortunately, depending on your perspective), Ford II was able to subject his will on the board and fire Iacocca. His other explanation of the determination not to quit was less honorable. Iacocca explained that greed—his personal quest to earn a $1 million annual salary—was also at the root of his decision. Furthermore, he enjoyed the automotive industry and, barring Henry Ford II, he loved his job. Some critics argue that Iacocca was ridiculously stubborn to continue at Ford under those conditions. Granted, Iacocca can be a stubborn man, but in this case he was convinced that not only did the company need him, but that he was right.

The conflict which culminated in his controversial and high-profile termination, had a dramatic affect on Iacocca's family. His wife, Mary and their two daughters understood that Lee was under intense stress but his firing was still a shock. Lia, his youngest daughter, away at tennis camp, actually learned of the news from the radio. Although unavoidable by her father, Lia was hurt by the impersonal method in which she was informed. The stress accumulated in Mary as well; diagnosed with diabetes, she suffered a heart attack less than three months after her husband was fired. Although the stress and pain were difficult for his family, they supported him and his decisions. As with Iacocca, all people who have enjoyed success, there is always a friend, spouse or family who's support and encouragement made the success possible. The bitter component of the termination for Iacocca was that it hurt the people he cared for the most.

Lee Iacocca spent 32 years of his life at the Ford Motor Company before his career was painfully and abruptly ended. His vision (leadership) to create the Mustang and the decisiveness (management) to produce it, is an excellent example of the need for leaders to be both efficient and effective. Although his strong resiliency could not prevail at Ford, it is an inspirational story. Supplemented by his ensuing success at Chrysler, it demonstrates that a leader with ability and a resilient character is limited only by the scope of his or her vision.

TRYING TIMES AT CHRYSLER

In 1978 it was no secret that the Chrysler Corporation was in trouble. Because Chrysler's cars had significantly dropped in quality, the company's market share had plummeted making it a distant third in the United States. When Iacocca was fired from Ford, many pundits immediately speculated that he would join Chrysler; indeed, it seemed a perfect match. But what the "experts", Iacocca and even Chrysler management failed to understand was the depth and scope of the company's troubles. As future events would prove, Chrysler's problems were so plentiful, severe and diverse that it was nearly impossible to save the company.

Talks between the Chrysler board of directors and the freshly unemployed Iacocca progressed quickly. Iacocca had offers from many other corporations including Radio Shack, International Paper and Lockheed and a few business schools approached him to become their dean. However, his life had been spent in the automobile business, and he didn't "know" the other industries.

Lee Iacocca did not desire to join Chrysler for the money or the fame; although he might have missed the limelight, financially he was set for life. Rather, he had three reasons for accepting the job. First, Iacocca wanted to join Chrysler because he was determined not to let his distinguished career end on a sour note. Still bitter at Ford II, he viewed Chrysler as a constructive opportunity to retaliate against his former boss. His revenge would come through developing better products and selling more cars to grab a portion of Ford's market share. Second, Iacocca believed he was too young to retire. He could have spent the rest of his life in comfortable fashion traveling and playing golf. Importantly, however, Iacocca still wanted to *do something* rather than look for *something to do*. This is a significant distinction and a characteristic shared by all effective leaders.

The final reason Iacocca had for joining Chrysler was that, like the other leaders in this book, he still desired a challenge. For Susan Anthony the challenge was to include women in the system and obtain their political, social and economic equality. For Harry Truman the challenge was to rebuild Europe and prevent a third world war. John Kennedy emphasized that he welcomed the challenge to revive and energize the dormant American spirit. Iacocca viewed the challenge to save an ailing American corporation whose bankruptcy would have meant the loss of hundreds of thousands of jobs. Iacocca, however, underestimated the enormity of this challenge.

At age 54, Lee Anthony Iacocca accepted the presidency of Chrysler in November of 1978 and proved to be the right person for the job. Clearly had he not possessed a vision, decisiveness and especially resiliency, Chrysler would have sunk even faster than the Titanic.

The First Year

In 1978, Chrysler, the nation's 10th largest company, lost $205 million, which in the ensuing years would seem like small potatoes. Iacocca's vision prior to assuming the job at Chrysler was to build the highest quality cars and trucks in the business to compete with Ford, General Motors and the Japanese so that Chrysler could again be profitable.   There were cars that he wanted to build at Ford incorporating state-of-the-art fuel efficiency and front wheel drive, but Ford II vetoed them.   Chrysler gave him a new opportunity, but to accomplish this, he would have to employ the decisiveness and innovation he exercised with the Mustang, Mark III and Fiesta.

He accepted the presidency of Chrysler under the condition that within a year he would also be made chairman and CEO. Iacocca believed that only with absolute control could he implement his management style and organize the system to meet his needs. As the "boss," he could steer the company in the direction of his vision. Unfortunately, it was not that simple for Iacocca. The situation was worse than anyone—including the top Chrysler management and board of directors—could imagine.

Internal communication and cohesion were Chrysler's greatest problems.   Each of the company's 35 vice presidents worked independent from the others with virtually no communication between them. It was very similar to Feudal England with lords and dukes only concerned with their little world and "ruling" their own area of the company. To Iacocca's surprise and chagrin, there was no coordination between the separate departments of production, engineering, marketing, manufacturing and sales. Design flaws, manufacturing inconsistencies simply were lost in the system. This led not only to an inferior product, but also to a large corporate debt due to cost overruns

Compounding these problems, Chrysler had no central financial controls; each department paid its bills out of the general fund. This made it difficult to figure out how much money was spent on any given product or process. This created two large problems: it was impossible to control or cut costs and there was no way to project or plan for the future. The departments also were not given budgets which made it literally impossible to over-spend.

The inferior product also was taking its toll on the company. Cars were falling apart as soon as they were purchased which caused sales to plummet. Since sales and production did not communicate, cars continued to roll off the assembly line. This led to a huge "sales bank" where many thousands of new cars deteriorated in parking lots. The company was not taking orders for cars, so the dealers had to sell the cars the company decided to make. This meant customers could not order the color, style and options they desired—their choices were usually limited to the cars the dealer happened to have on the lot. Clearly, Chrysler Corporation was in a state of anarchy.

In contrast to President Harry Truman's situation concerning the Korean War, Iacocca was in big trouble. Truman's situation was serious and threatening, but he had an organization geared to the decision making process which quickly provided him with all the necessary information. Iacocca, on the other hand, could not even determine exactly where Chrysler was losing money. Individual plants did not even submit profit/loss statements. With this huge, complex mess, Iacocca had no starting place to cut costs or plan for the future—the system prevented him, and everyone else, from forming a perspective. Thus, for the new company president, it was not a matter of simply figuring out how to save the company (although that was extremely complex in itself). He first had to establish a system of controls and communication so that he could gather the necessary information to form an action plan to save the company. To make matters even worse, with each passing day, Chrysler fell deeper and deeper into an abyss of debt.

Iacocca realized that the situation had deteriorated too far for one person to fix. He needed a lot of help from experienced and efficient managers. Jerry Greenwald and Steve Miller defected from Ford to put the financial control system in order. To clean up the sales bank fiasco and smooth relations between Chrysler and its dealers, Iacocca hired Gar Laux, an ex-Ford man in semi-retirement.

Iacocca coaxed Hans Matthias out of retirement to reorganize and control the manufacturing system, and Paul Bergmoser was hired to revamp purchasing. Also added to the new team were George Butts, Steve Sharf and Dick Dauch who significantly impacted Chrysler's faulty quality control system. Additionally, each person brought several hungry executives eager for a challenge. They came from Ford, Volkswagen, General Motors, Fiat and a few that were already employed at Chrysler.

Hal Sperlich, who was fired from Ford a few years earlier, was already designing products at Chrysler when Iacocca joined the company. While Iacocca was drastically cutting spending and lowering overhead throughout the company, he gave Sperlich free reign to develop new cars and trucks. Chrysler spent hundreds of millions of dollars in this area because Iacocca realized its importance. He understood that without new, innovative and quality products three to five years down the line that any short term turnaround would be worthless. In short, the present was a waste of time if there was to be no future. This was an important investment by Iacocca.

Perhaps the biggest shakeup, however, was in marketing. Iacocca released the two ad agencies employed by Chrysler and replaced them with Kenyon & Eckhardt. K & E had been his agency at Ford and they understood his methods, desires and style. By bringing them in, he did not spend precious time acquainting himself with new agencies.

With his team reorganizing the entire company, Iacocca set his sights on the consumer. The biggest problem for Chrysler was that the public viewed its products as inferior. Even after his team corrected many of the problems, the perception still existed. This required Iacocca and K & E to be innovative. To show the consumer that quality actually had improved, the company invited them to test-drive a Chrysler. If they ended up buying a car from a competitor, Chrysler gave them $50. Another innovation was the unconditional guarantee. If a customer did not like the car he purchased for any reason, he could bring it back within 30 days for a refund. These programs brought thousands of people into the showrooms. Because customers could see for themselves that the products were of a much improved quality, they cost Chrysler very little money.

With the quality of cars improving, the organizational controls and systems being implemented and the investment in the future made, Iacocca was in a position to bring Chrysler back into the black.

The Savior

Under those conditions, Iacocca probably could have saved the company without outside assistance. Unfortunately, the conditions changed again—for the worse. In 1979 the Iranian Revolution forced the Shah out of Tehran and into exile in the United States. The anti-American sentiments in the Middle East precipitated an oil embargo and the price of gasoline in the United States doubled. Until 1979 American automakers could not build full-size cars fast enough to meet consumer demands. The overnight energy crunch created a massive shift to smaller, more fuel efficient cars. This was one outside influence Iacocca would have to deal with.

Unbelievably, the situation grew worse for Chrysler as interest rates soared and the country plunged into a recession. New car sales were down nearly 50 percent and Chrysler's market share dipped to an all-time low of eight percent. Clearly it was going to take drastic measures to revive Chrysler.

The first of these was to raise cash. Iacocca began by selling any part of the company that did not directly relate to producing and selling cars. This included real estate, their division producing tanks for the army, and their operations in all foreign countries except Mexico and Canada. This, however, was not enough; Iacocca had to reduce costs. Within the first two years Iacocca was at Chrysler, over 15,000 salaried workers lost their jobs. Additionally, he was forced to close several plants which cost thousands of blue-collar workers their jobs. Having recently been fired himself, this was an emotionally difficult task for Iacocca. It wasn't pleasant, but the alternative was that *everyone* lost their job.

Through these stressful and frustrating times, Iacocca was able to stay focused and determined. Regardless of how bad the situation grew, he kept his vision in mind of a rebuilt and healthy Chrysler Corporation. This illustrates a vital interrelationship between a vision and the need for a resilient character. Without this vision of a better and brighter future, Iacocca could not have displayed the necessary resiliency. Without resiliency, he probably would have quit when the going was rough—long before the vision was realized.

Given the recession, energy crisis and chaotic internal situation of the company, Iacocca and Chrysler had three options to survive. First, they could secure conventional loans and borrow their way out of the mess, but debt was one of Chrysler's larger problems. Chrysler already owed $4.75 billion and was having difficulty making the payments on the existing loans. The company's situation and the state of the economy made it nearly impossible to find lending institutions willing to take such a risk. Further conventional loans, therefore, were out of the question.

The second option for Chrysler and Iacocca was to file for bankruptcy. Under such a plan, the company would have been protected from its creditors until it was reorganized and profitable. But Chrysler's situation was unique. Bankruptcy would have destroyed the company very quickly because it would have placed doubt and fear in the minds of consumers. People would simply not purchase a Chrysler car or truck if there was a good chance the company would not be around to service and honor the warrantee of the car. In fact, the hints, rumors and speculation of a Chrysler bankruptcy were partially responsible for the company's dismal sales figures. Bankruptcy, therefore, was not a viable option for Chrysler.

The final option for Iacocca and Chrysler was to seek guaranteed loans from the federal government. Realizing this was the only hope for his dying company, Iacocca approached Uncle Sam. This course of action sparked a large and heated national debate. Because the government would be assisting a failed business in its free market economy, there was considerable opposition to the plan. It was also in direct contradiction to what Iacocca and many other businessmen had advocated for years: governmental regulation was killing American business. It now appeared that Iacocca had changed his mind and was asking government to interfere in free enterprise. Opponents of the plan were concerned that bailing out Chrysler would set a dangerous precedent because it, in effect, rewarded failure. While expounding "survival of the fittest" arguments, opponents asserted that Chrysler's failure was actually in the best interest of the United States because it reinforced the idea that a company which was poorly managed and produced inferior products should and would fail. This, they argued, was healthy for the country.

Iacocca testified before House and Senate committees to gain support for the plan and to dispel the numerous rumors and myths. His main premise was that the government was partially responsible for the company's failure. In conjunction with poor management, governmental regulation had created a great strain on the company. For one long week, Iacocca explained to anyone in Washington who would listen that pollution control standards, safety regulations and fuel efficiency requirements had cost Chrysler $1 billion in the previous two years. Additionally, anti-trust laws prohibited the three American automakers from pooling their research and development efforts in these areas. The redundancy and enormous costs, Iacocca concluded, were most detrimental to Chrysler, the smallest of the "Big Three" American car makers.

Iacocca also explained to Congress that loan guarantees to Chrysler would not be setting a precedent. In fact, the United States government had granted similar guarantees to steel companies, airlines, students, tobacco growers, ship builders, New York City and companies in most other American industries. The amount of these loans totaled $409 billion—Chrysler was asking for a mere $1.2 billion. Iacocca was trying to convince Congress and the American people that Chrysler was not breaking new ground with the request, and to be fair, the government should grant the loans.

The final component of Iacocca's message was particularly persuasive. He had prepared a detailed list of where the 600,000 jobs would be lost if his company was to go bankrupt. Because the company's dealers, plants and suppliers were scattered throughout the country, Chrysler's demise would have negatively impacted 433 of the 435 Congressional districts. Iacocca predicted that the government would have to pay over $16 billion in unemployment benefits to this huge workforce. Iacocca further asserted that the government was at no financial risk by granting the $1.2 billion loan because Chrysler's assets were worth at least $2.7 billion and the government would be repaid before banks and other creditors. Thus the debate was reduced largely to ideology—free enterprise versus government interference. The tragedy was that the livelihood of over a half a million families hinged on the decision. Finally, in December of 1979, Congress approved the bailout by a large majority in the House and a slim margin in the Senate. Chrysler, however, still had a few hurdles to clear before it could receive the loan and continue business.

To prevent all failing businesses from running to their rich uncle, Congress stipulated that the process was to be as difficult and unpleasant as reasonably possible. Therefore, for the loan to be granted, Chrysler had to obtain concessions from its workers, the United Auto Workers (UAW) and from its creditors. To demonstrate what he called "equality of sacrifice" Iacocca reduced his salary to $1 a year. In this way, he showed the UAW that everyone would have to make sacrifices to save the company. This gesture won him the respect of workers, executives and the American public as a traditional "fat cat" had really given of himself to make the plan work. Impressed by Iacocca's action and faced with the proposition of unemployment, the UAW agreed to accept a $2 per hour pay cut.

Banks represented the opposite end of the spectrum making it very difficult for Chrysler. Each bank had to agree to forgive a certain percentage of their loans and extend the company more credit. This created an enormous uproar and many institutions were adamantly opposed to the plan. Each gave several reasons why it should not have to sacrifice while the others should. Iacocca maintained a hard line approach that all institutions, regardless of the amount of the loan, would sacrifice an equal percentage. Iacocca also pointed out to the banks that their only alternative was to sue the company after it declared bankruptcy and years later receive pennies on the dollar.   Eventually, after months of negotiations, disagreements and ultimatums, the banks agreed and Chrysler received its first installment of $500 million.

The K-car was the vehicle that saved the Chrysler Corporation. It was the car Hal Sperlich had begun work on immediately after he joined the company in 1977 and the car Iacocca believed to be Chrysler's last hope. Without his substantial investment when cash was tight and his unconditional support of Sperlich, the company would have had nothing competitive to sell after it received the government loans. Iacocca's foresight and vision reaped great dividends as the K-car was responsible for Chrysler turning a profit in 1982. Chrysler's $3.5 billion in losses from the previous four years was forgotten in the success, and on August 15, 1983, eight years ahead of schedule, Chrysler repaid the government the entire loan. It took five years, but Iacocca had realized his vision: Chrysler was once again a strong, healthy and competitive company.

Iacocca's vision was responsible for the turnaround. Without a vision he could have faltered at many points of the four year struggle. With his vision in mind he was able to remind himself that the success of the company superseded the immediate needs of the UAW, the banks and even his own salary. It was a guiding force and an inspiration when it would have been much easier for him to quit than to face the embarrassment and frustration of asking Congress to bail out his company. His vision also gave him the strength to be resilient as the company crumbled around him and when he thought he had finally hit rock bottom and things got even worse.

Throughout his 32 years with Ford and career at Chrysler, Iacocca displayed exceptional management skills. But his success illustrates, more than any other leader profiled in this book, that leadership is a different skill than management. Efficient management propelled him quickly to the top of the company; effective leadership was responsible for his success at the top. While we help our managers to become leaders, we must also help our leaders to become managers. If the United States can do this, the resulting leadership literate workforce will be both efficient and effective.

Chapter 5

Martin Luther King, Jr.

No one person has made such a significant impact on American society in his or her first 39 years of life as did Martin Luther King, Jr. In the brief time of 13 years, King awakened a nation to its unjust and shameful treatment of 18 million of its citizens. King not only exposed and publicized the social ills of segregation and racism, but he was able to make the system begin to correct itself. Making his feats more difficult, he was in constant physical danger; he received threats and hate mail while racists and opponents of change stabbed, bombed and beat King and his followers. King's two great leadership qualities—resiliency and vision—kept the movement strong, committed and on course to achieve racial equality in the United States. Our country has by no means fulfilled his dream, but without his leadership the civil rights movement could have resulted in a bloody conflict between the races, widening even further the existing ideological gap.

Martin and Alberta King's second child, Martin Luther King, Jr., was born January 15, 1929 in Atlanta, Georgia. Martin Sr. was the minister of the Ebenezer Baptist Church—the parish his father-in-law, Alfred Daniel Williams, founded and ministered. The Kings were a middle class family with traditional values of religion, family and education. As young children, Martin (known as "M.L."), his older sister, Christine and younger brother Alfred Daniel (known as "A.D"), played with several neighborhood children of whom some were white. As they became school-age, however, the white children were no longer permitted to play with the Kings and the other black children. This was the first of many encounters King would have with segregation in the South.

Segregation had been a way of life in the South since the demise of slavery. Although the Emancipation Proclamation freed the slaves upon the Confederate surrender, the new citizens were never integrated into American society. During Reconstruction, many blacks were elected to local, state and federal offices, but violence and the passage of Jim Crow laws led to rigid segregation within a generation. Blacks were prevented for voting, receiving a fair trial and sharing public facilities with whites. This not only caused physical and emotional harm to black Americans, but the affects of the economic poverty and educational deficiencies it created are still felt today. The 1896 *Plessy V. Fergusen* Supreme Court decision established the "separate but equal" doctrine as the law of the land. With segregation came a degradation and a constant label as a second class citizen. Challenges of this order were met promptly with violence. Even children were not free from these dangers: A Northern black youth playfully whistled at a white woman while visiting relatives in the South. Word soon spread of the event, and the boy's brutally beaten body was found the next day. Countless lynchings, rapes, castrations and other horrible acts of violence were committed against black Americans—even in the twentieth century--to preserve the segregated way of life. The Ku Klux Klan, hooded soldiers of hatred and bigotry, used, and continue to use, fear and violence to promote the "white supremacy" doctrine. The North was not free from the disease of prejudice; employment, education and housing discrimination were common practice in many Northern cities, and even to this day, the Klan maintains chapters throughout the country.

M.L. was an exceptionally bright young man and a gifted student. He skipped three grades and graduated from high school at the age of 15. He enrolled at Morehouse College in Atlanta to become a doctor or a lawyer. The influence of religion and his father, in conjunction with his great talent for public speaking, eventually sparked his interest in seminary studies. After he graduated from Morehouse in 1948, he enrolled in the Crozer Theological Seminary at Bucknell University in Chester, Pennsylvania. Although he received many scholarship offers, King chose Crozer because it was one of the nation's best theological schools. He achieved a straight-A average at Crozer but he also found success outside the classrooms; he was elected student-body president. King enjoyed the freedom of the North. Although contact and conversation between the races was kept to a minimum, theaters, restaurants and virtually all public and most private facilities were integrated.

It was at Crozer that King was introduced to the principles of nonviolent protest practiced by Mohandas K. Gandhi of India. King was soon confronted with an opportunity to practice the nonviolence he was studying. A common prank of the time was to enter a classmate's room in his absence and overturn the beds, desks and chairs before the victim returned. These harmless practical jokes were executed by everyone including King. On one occasion, the victim was from North Carolina and had difficulty accepting King and other blacks as peers. Upon discovering the prank he confronted King, and in anger he threatened King with a pistol. Calmly King informed the victim that he had not been one of the pranksters. He finally put the gun away and a tragedy was averted. In a strong display of nonviolent principles, King refused to press charges against his classmate. At the urging of the university, the student eventually offered King a public apology. King's calm and mature reaction to the danger and his forgiving attitude won the admiration and praise of both the student body and the faculty.

During his time at Crozer, hatred and racism spurred another unpleasant incident which demonstrated to King that racial prejudice toward blacks was not confined to the South. One evening he was on a double date with his friend Walter McCall. They decided to stop at a restaurant near Camden, New Jersey and have something to eat. The foursome was ignored by the waitress. Upon asking the manager, they were told that they would not be served. King, McCall and their dates left the establishment but soon returned with a police officer who arrested the manager for violating an anti-discrimination law. The case was prosecuted by the NAACP, but a lack of "objective evidence" resulted in its dismissal.

King graduated from Crozer as the class valedictorian in 1951 and was awarded a $1200 scholarship to continue his studies. He enrolled at Boston University as a Ph.D. candidate where his area of interest would be the value of human personality, or personalism. Boston University was a leading institution in this relatively new field of philosophy. King and his roommate, Philip Lenud, organized the Philosophical Club; one evening a week, students would gather to discuss and debate many different subjects of philosophy. Often students would read papers they had written and then welcome criticism. These debates frequently lasted well into the morning hours.

Education greatly enhanced the life of Martin Luther King, Jr. as he was an incredibly interesting and complex man. He had the fortune of a diverse background—a Southern Christian childhood and a Northern liberal education. Thus, the well-rounded King was able to relate well to poor and middle class blacks in the South and to the white middle and upper classes of the North. King's education enabled him to apply this knowledge by fitting it into the context of the vast underlying social, political and economic forces at work in the United States. Because he could grasp both the specifics and the "big picture" of the civil rights movement, he was more capable to effect change.

One of King's most important discoveries during his years at Boston University, however, was of a social nature. Through a mutual friend, King met Coretta Scott who was studying at the New England Conservatory of Music in Boston. Coretta Scott was determined to have a career of her own and was somewhat cool to the idea of marriage. But she soon realized that Martin was the right man for her. He assured her that as the wife of a minister she would not have to give up her singing career. The two were married by Martin's father on June 18, 1953 at the Scott family home in Marion, Alabama. Because both still had to complete their degrees, they rented an apartment in Boston the next school-year.

Pending the conferment of his degree, three colleges had offered King excellent positions ranging from administration to faculty. In addition, two churches—one in Massachusetts, the other in New York—had asked him to be their minister. Martin, Sr. had been grooming Martin, Jr. to take his place at the Atlanta church. Also, King received a letter from the officers of a church in

Montgomery, Alabama. Although they were without a minister, they had not offered him the job. For what could be described as an audition, the Dexter Street Baptist Church asked King to deliver a sermon. King agreed and the date was set for a Sunday in January. The Dexter Street Baptist Church had largely a black middle class congregation, similar to that of his father's church in Atlanta. His sermon "The Three Dimensions of a Complete Life" was a great success, and the church officers made him their unanimous choice to fill their vacancy. After much thought and discussion with his wife, King decided to return to the South and accept the offer.

His decision to become the Dexter Street Baptist Church minister was the most important decision of his career. If King had decided to stay in the North or to become a professor, he would have had much less of an opportunity to impact to civil rights movement. As a minister, he did not rely on the white establishment for a job, house or other support. The autonomy of having these furnished by a black congregation gave him, and other ministers, the opportunity to become "agitators" and expose the injustices of segregation. Those depending on whites for their livelihood could quickly find themselves without a job if they challenged the system. This is why the civil rights movement was influenced so greatly by the religious establishment.

In the following year, King was thrust into leadership as Rosa Parks was arrested for refusing to give her bus seat to a white passenger. King was successful in leading the Montgomery bus boycott because he implemented the principles of nonviolence. This method would become his trademark and the successes he achieved through it made him a national figure.

After the Montgomery success, he helped form the Southern Christian Leadership Conference, SCLC, which facilitated civil rights protest and progress throughout the South. In 1963, King and the SCLC organized a march on Washington DC to lobby Congress where he delivered his famous "I Have a Dream" speech. In 1964 he won the Nobel Peace Prize for his nonviolent protests and his overall message of peace and understanding between the races.

King's goal was to make Americans and the entire world aware of a great irony in the United States: injustice and oppression were thriving in the most free nation on Earth. King's nonviolent method was not to point fingers and lay blame on persons acting unjustly as they advanced segregation, rather he tried to love and understand them and reform the unjust system itself. Punishment and judgement, King believed, were for the courts and the historians. King's leadership style was a blend of the resiliency of Susan B. Anthony and the visionary and communicative abilities of John F. Kennedy. This potent combination of leadership characteristics made King, perhaps, the greatest all-around leader to live in the past 125 years.

THE DREAM

Of all his accomplishments, Martin Luther King, Jr. is best remembered for the historic "I Have a Dream" speech he delivered in the summer of 1963. His "dream" became a symbol of the movement because it was a visionary appeal to create a better future—one with which his followers could identify. In terms of vision, King and John Kennedy were the masters of this century. Although other public figures and politicians have formulated visionary programs and approaches to problems, one important fact separates them from the stature of King and Kennedy: these two exceptional leaders' eloquent rhetoric and captivating speeches were supported with substance and vigorous action directly leading to success. Kennedy acquired the funds, persuaded the passage of legislation and gained the public support necessary to accomplish his goals. In the same way, King raised the necessary funds, organized the protests, requested the legislative support and even went to jail on numerous occasions to ensure the success of his cause. King's visionary greatness lay in his message, his language and the credibility he accrued throughout the movement.

King's message was that the future of America and the black race would be better than the present situation. He believed that an

America could be created where racism, violence, hatred and oppression would just be memories. Although he had communicated his vision to many people in many different places and in many different ways, his *I Have a Dream* speech most effectively and most eloquently summarized his ideal and unique image of the future. Envisioned King:

> I say to you today, my friends, that in spite of the difficulties and frustrations of the moment, I still have a dream. It is a dream deeply rooted in the American dream.
>
> I have a dream that one day this nation will rise up and live out the true meaning of its creed: "We hold these truths to be self-evident; that all men are created equal."
>
> I have a dream that one day on the red hills of Georgia the sons of former slaves and the sons of former slaveowners will be able to sit down together at the table of brotherhood.
>
> I have a dream that one day even the state of Mississippi, a desert state sweltering with the heat of injustice and oppression, will be transformed into an oasis of freedom and justice.
>
> I have a dream that my four little children will one day live in a nation where they will not be judged by the color of their skin but by the content of their character.
>
> I have a dream today.
>
> I have a dream that one day the state of Alabama, whose governor's lips are presently dripping with the words of interposition and nullification, will be transformed into a situation where little black boys and little black girls will be able to join hands with little white boys and little white girls and walk together as sisters and brothers.
>
> I have a dream today.
>
> I have a dream that one day every valley shall be exalted, every hill and mountain shall be made low, the rough places will be made plain, and the crooked places will be made straight, and the glory of the Lord shall be revealed, and all flesh shall see it together.

On another occasion he spoke of his vision, but warned that the path leading there would be difficult to climb. In November of

1961 he gave a speech to the Fellowship of the Concerned that was reminiscent of John Kennedy's "New Frontier" speech. King explained:

> . . . this movement is a movement based on faith in the future. It is a movement based on a philosophy, the possibility of the future bringing into being something real and something meaningful. It is a movement based on hope. I think this is very important. . .
>
> And I think this should be a challenge to all others who are struggling to transform the dangling discords of our Southland into a beautiful symphony of brotherhood. There is something in this . . . movement which says to us, that we shall overcome. Before the victory is won some may have to get scarred up, but we shall overcome. Before the victory of brotherhood is achieved, some will face physical death, but we shall overcome. Before the victory is won, some will lose jobs, some will be called Communists, and reds, merely because they believe in brotherhood, some will be dismissed as dangerous rabble-rousers and agitators merely because they're standing up for what's right, but we shall overcome. . .
>
> With this faith in the future, with this determined struggle, we will be able to emerge from the bleak and desolate midnight of man's inhumanity to man, into the bright and glittering daybreak of freedom and justice.

Similar to John Kennedy, King promised not what he could give to his followers, but promised that through their mutual struggle and effort, they could create a greater America. In this way, their vision inspired others to action; followers could see the advantages of the described future and believed it to be worth the sacrifice.

If civil rights were purely a rational issue, the simple argument of justice and equality for all Americans would have affected the change. Although many Americans were swayed by this argument, many were not. For them it was not a rational issue—it was wrapped in emotion. Because civil rights reform challenged their heritage, sense of tradition and entire belief structure, it was too powerful to deal with rationally. The notion of racial equality challenged the unfounded beliefs and myths of the black race's inherent inferiority ingrained by centuries of slavery and segregation. Many humans do not react rationally to change; to them it is viewed as inherently bad. Thus, our reaction to change can be irrational and controlled by emotion. This partially explains why King met such violent and wide-spread resistance. Although his message would never appeal to some, for many it did appeal both to their sense of reason and to their emotions. This was an important factor in his success.

The language used by King, and Kennedy, was fresh and exciting. They both employed active verbs and numerous patriotic references while they harnessed the power of terse phrasing and stylistic devices. King also filled his speeches and writings with religious references because his movement was largely comprised of a people deeply devoted to Christianity. His ability to extemporaneously quote from the Bible and draw parallels between the movement's situation and those of Biblical personalities, made for a greater understanding of his ideas. It also was a form of emotional appeal, as religion is based on faith and beliefs that do not relate well to conventional wisdom.

The metaphor, however, was the most effective component of his language. Metaphors help an audience create a mental image of where the leader's vision will lead and what the situation will look like when they have achieved it. King's artistic use of metaphor throughout his *I Have a Dream* speech enabled his supporters and critics to better visualize his message. Because his audiences were able to understand his ideas and vision, they were more apt to accept them. The persuasion inherent in all communication can be greatly enhanced by the effective use of metaphor, stylistic devices and fresh, active and exciting language. This draws attention to and wins acceptance of a leader's vision.

King's credibility greatly increased the effectiveness of his vision. His behavior throughout his active involvement in the civil rights movement was of the highest ethical standards. King was viewed as credible for four reasons. First, much violence was directed at him. He was punched, kicked, beaten, stabbed and ultimately killed for his participation and leadership of the movement. In each case, he reacted nonviolently to the aggressor. This enabled him to ask others to sacrifice in the same way. Would-be victims of the violence inflicted on demonstrators were much more likely to participate for a leader who knew for himself the pains, sacrifices and frustrations of being a victim.

The second reason King was viewed as credible was his great intellect and impressive education. Few blacks were fortunate enough to have the opportunity to attend college, especially in the South. King's Ph.D. earned him additional respect.

Third, King was successful. People would follow him and work to achieve his vision because he had previously been successful in defeating segregation and they believed that with their help, he could do it again. Montgomery was his first success, but Birmingham, the march on Washington D.C. and the Selma-Montgomery march all contributed to his stature as an effective leader.

The final reason King was viewed as credible was that he did not abuse his power. Countless opportunities existed for him to use SCLC funds and monetary donations for his private use, but King was above that. In fact, he gave the entire $54,600 prize money for his Nobel Peace Prize to the movement. The FBI and IRS extensively probed his personal finances, but neither organization could produce evidence that King ever acted improperly. King realized, as did Susan Anthony, that it was imperative to act with the highest integrity. Any breach of ethics would draw the national attention away from the quest of achieving the vision and focus it on an ugly scandal. This would not only have hurt him, but it would have been detrimental to the cause.

To better understand the context of King's dream, it is important to note the influence of the Black Muslim movement in the United States. Unlike King's approach, the Black Muslims and Malcolm X, one of their most prominent ministers, advocated retaliatory violence and preached a hatred and contempt for the white race. As King advocated action through nonviolence, Malcolm X inspired many Northern blacks to vent their anger and frustration through violence. While King's nonviolent protests throughout the South often resulted in violence, usually instigated by the segregationists, Malcolm X and Black Muslims encouraged riots and violent conflicts in many Northern cities.

Malcolm X, however, was an exceptional leader in his own right. Born Malcolm Little, he was a perfect example of a Northern Black being pushed through the cracks of the system by the white establishment. Although the brightest and most popular of his integrated grade school, his teacher told him that he could not be a doctor or lawyer—that he ought to instead be a carpenter. Eventually Malcolm X turned to crime and spent time in prison where he was introduced to the Islamic faith and joined the Black Muslims. His stance on the race issue drastically changed after he made a pilgrimage to Mecca, the Islamic holy city, in 1964. This caused him to split with the Black Muslim Church and form his own faith—Muslim Mosque, Inc. In 1965 he explained to Coretta King the rationale for his aggressive and often violent approach to the race issue, " . . .I didn't come to make (Dr. King's) job more difficult. I thought that if white people understood what the alternative was that they would be willing to listen to Dr. King."

Although not formally planned or rehearsed, the diametrically opposed approaches of King and Malcolm X affected the nation much like that of a "good cop-bad cop" scenario. As Malcolm X preached violence, separation and black supremacy, King soothed with words of peace and the ideas of justice, unity and brotherhood. Malcolm X appealed to a different audience than King. King's education and experience enabled him to relate well to nearly every demographic group except the Northern urban poor blacks. The ghetto was where Malcolm X enjoyed his greatest support. Because he had lived there and experienced the frustration, he could express their feelings and address their needs better than King. Without Malcolm X's influence frightening many politicians and their constituencies into action, King's dream might not have not enjoyed as many successes.

The Black Muslims and Malcolm X made one other important and often overlooked contribution to the civil rights movement and to the black race. After centuries of forced servitude, most black Americans were unaware of their black roots in Africa. Malcolm X taught black Americans about their African heritage; they came from an important culture that was responsible for the origins of the human race. Malcolm X and African history scholars told of a beautiful and proud people ruled by great kings who enjoyed the arts and the lifestyle of an advanced culture. Both King and Malcolm X (at the end of his career) operated under the assumption that the black and white races were created equal. But Malcolm X, unlike King, perceived that many blacks themselves, due to centuries of degradation, did not believe in their racial equality. In this way, Malcolm X addressed a different need of the black race— the need for a positive self image and a boosted self esteem. The black pride exalted by Malcolm X was an important step for the black race in believing for themselves that they were not an inferior race.

WE SHALL OVERCOME

The civil rights movement of the 1950s and 1960s was a violent period in the history of the United States. The Ku Klux Klan and other organizations advancing white supremacy and segregation terrorized black Americans throughout the country. Lynchings, beatings, bombings, murders and other acts of senseless violence were commonplace. The emotional abuse inflicted was sometimes just as cruel and painful as the physical damage. But it is impossible for a person who did not experience this shameful treatment to adequately explain it or to fully empathize with those who did. To endure single acts of degradation and violence took a strong will. To withstand them and feel the fear, anger and hopelessness on a daily and constant basis took a powerful resiliency. To be a leader in a social reform movement plagued by violence proves to be the greatest test of one's character, determination and resiliency. This was the test posed to Martin Luther King, Jr. and black America by the Jim Crow laws and the segregationist and racist institutions existing in America. "We Shall Overcome" became the anthem of the civil rights movement. This spiritual song has its roots in the pre-Civil War era of American history; it was sung by black Americans as they looked to and hoped for a brighter future for their enslaved race.

The resiliency displayed by King in his crusade for civil rights progress and justice in the American system is not unlike that exhibited by Susan B. Anthony in her lifelong struggle for woman's rights. The differences between Iacocca and Anthony are very similar to those between Iacocca and King. The difference is in the circumstances; the similarity is in the fact that neither would quit when the situation got rough. A comparison of the resiliency displayed by King and Anthony is particularly enlightening as we further our understanding of the characteristic.

It is first necessary, however, to understand the similarities and differences of their respective movements before a contrast and comparison of their resilient characters can be appreciated. Both King and Anthony became the leader, more or less, of a movement advocating social reform to include a neglected class of citizens in the American system. From our vantage point in the 1990s, we can see that both were "doing the right thing" and had true justice on their side. Both praised and respected the American form of government despite its flaws. King, unlike Anthony, had to endure both the verbal and physical attacks and abuse. Susan B. Anthony was often ridiculed and degraded but, not devaluing her accomplishments, she, unlike King, was never in any physical danger from the white male establishment. King had the advantage (or disadvantage) of technology and a mass media to communicate and spread his message while Anthony had to rely on the press in the slow, pre-electronic age. Technology also made communication internal to the movement much easier for King. The telephone, automobile and airplane were significant advantages over the telegraph and stagecoach. But just as they were an asset to King, proponents of segregation also had technology at their disposal.

In terms of resiliency, both were exceptional models, but each had a distinctive style and method. Anthony became involved in the woman's rights movement while in her 30s and continued until her death at 86 years old. King was thrust into leadership at the age of 27 and was killed well before his prime at 39. Thus, King's resiliency was marked by youth and energy while Anthony's persistence for 50 years transformed the characteristics of her resiliency from youthful energy into a resolved and determined silver-haired stateswoman. Although both were willing—and did— go to jail for their respective causes, Susan B. Anthony saw very few victories in her lifelong struggle. While it could be argued that Anthony was ahead of her time, timing was King's greatest fortune—the existing social conditions in the 1950 and 1960s made victories possible in the civil rights movement.

In times of despair, a resilient leader must look somewhere for strength and inspiration; while Anthony looked to herself, King turned to God for the energy and conviction to continue. King's Achilles heel was his self-confidence. While no person may ever be "ready" for leadership at a national level, King, at 27 years old, was qualified, yet unproven. The youthful King needed the successes of the movement, his faith in God, the support of his wife, and the words of encouragement of his peers and elders to remain a confident leader. His need for external confidence builders decreased as his career progressed, but the Montgomery bus boycott would test under-fire his leadership ability. As would most or all 27 year-olds in a similar position of enormous responsibility, King often found himself mired in self-doubt and plagued by guilt for setbacks. King, with the aid of his religious faith and the encouragement of Coretta and his fellow protestors, found the mental toughness and courage to continue. This inner struggle of one of America's greatest twentieth century leaders proves that no leader is without self-doubt and an occasional lack of confidence. The truly exceptional leaders, as was King, win their inner struggles and exercise their other leadership qualities.

Although their circumstances, causes and styles were diverse, both Anthony and King possessed the great resiliency necessary to lead their respective movements. Clearly, without their individual displays of mental toughness and wills to continue, twentieth century history would have been written much differently.

"Nonviolence" became the key word to characterize the civil rights movement under the leadership of Martin Luther King, Jr. To King there were six characteristics and benefits of the nonviolent approach to problems. First, the purpose of nonviolence is not humiliate or defeat the opposition; its goal is to win the opponent's friendship and understanding. Nonviolence works on the opponents sense of morality and its success is due to the shame felt by the opponent when reflecting on his or her violent actions. The results of violence are hatred and bitterness while nonviolence results in peace and harmony.

Second, nonviolence is not a "do nothing" approach—it is resistance, but passive only physically. Mohandas Gandhi, the Indian who led his country to independence from the British Empire, said that given the two alternatives—violence and cowardice—it is preferable to fight. Nonviolence is a distinctive third option.

The third characteristic of nonviolence is the focus of attack is not on the persons doing the evil, rather it is on the evil itself. This was one reason for the effectiveness of the Truman Committee—it directed its efforts to expose injustice, but it did not point fingers or attempt to prosecute individuals. Truman, like Gandhi, King and other employers of the nonviolent approach, labored to defeat injustice, not to defeat the individual persons who may have been acting unjustly.

The fourth, and perhaps most obvious, characteristic is the participants willingness to endure violence without retaliating through physical aggression. This important characteristic aids the first point in shaming the opponent into cooperation because it is easier to justify violence against someone who fights back. King also believed that the suffering nonviolence caused had redemptive value. Suffering, he felt, allowed the individual to become more introspective and thus, be a personally educational and transforming power.

The fifth characteristic of nonviolence is perhaps the most misunderstood. The nonviolent participant not only refuses to hate his or her opposition, but instead offers love. Many unfamiliar with the nonviolent method argue that it is not rational, or possible, to love someone who exerts such violence and hatred. King explained that the Greek language contains three words for, and thus defines, three different types of love. The first is *eros*—romantic love. *Philia*, meaning love between friends, or reciprocal love, is the second type. The third type, which concerns nonviolence, is *agape*. *Agape*, according to King, is an understanding and redemptive good will for humanity. *Agape* is the type of love that transforms hate and anger into an understanding and empathy of an opponent's perspective and motives. *Agape* partially explains a robbery victim forgiving the thief because he or she understands the perpetrators situation—the thief may be homeless, jobless or have fallen through the cracks of the system and is stealing only to provide food for himself and his family. Through *agape*, the victim seeks to gain an understanding of the circumstances and spends his or her energy to rectify or reform the underlying causes for the crime, not to punish the criminal.

The sixth characteristic of nonviolence is that it is based on the assumption and belief that ultimately justice will prevail. It is a strong spiritual faith that the forces at work in the universe are on the side of justice. This further explains the participant's willingness to suffer as he or she has a deep faith in a positive future.

These six characteristics, when fully understood and employed, make nonviolence an enormously powerful force for social, economic and political change. Gandhi's use of nonviolence in his country's quest for justice was a revelation to Western Civilization. He showed that war, violence and oppression are not the only means to effect mass social change. Furthermore, he showed that they are not, in fact, the most effective or preferred. King had studied and was convinced of the merits of the nonviolent method. Gandhi's triumph in India in the first half of the twentieth century provided a concrete example with which blacks could relate and through which they could better understand the concept. This made possible King's triumphs in the second half of the century.

The Montgomery Bus Boycott

If there was one single event that sparked the modern civil rights movement, it was Rosa Parks' refusal to give her bus seat to a white passenger in Montgomery, Alabama on December 1, 1955. Debate continues among scholars as to whether or not she was "planted" by the NAACP to make a test case of the city's segregation laws. Later the seamstress reported that she simply was tired after a long day of work and that her feet hurt. Whether or not she was a plant is irrelevant—the importance of her brave act of civil disobedience was the civil rights progress made as a result of her refusal and subsequent arrest. Her situation became a true representation of the feelings the black race had for their treatment in American society: black Americans were tired after three centuries of slavery, abuse, degradation and oppression. As Rosa Parks, the black race in America would no longer stand for the injustices.

In theory, the 1954 *Brown vs. Board of Education of Topeka* ruling of the Supreme Court had put an end to the "separate but equal" doctrine that had governed public education. It did not, however, outlaw racial segregation of other public facilities. Thus, in 1955 blacks were relegated to the rear of busses throughout the South. Signs marked "white" and "colored" were attached to the seats and moved further to the rear as the number of white passengers increased. They were constant and degrading reminders of where blacks were allowed to sit. Often, after paying their fare at the front of the bus, blacks were required to enter through the rear door so they would not walk by the white passengers seated in the front. Many times drivers actually drove away as blacks walked outside to enter the rear door.

As with any large social group, factions existed within the Montgomery black community. Upon hearing the news of Parks' arrest, the black leadership quickly set aside their differences and met Friday, December 2 to determine a response to the event. The Women's Political Council suggested a boycott of the entire Montgomery bus system by all black riders. The leaders were quickly united in agreement and a mass meeting was scheduled for that evening to inform the community of the plan. At this large gathering, ministers agreed to endorse the boycott at their Sunday services and the black-owned and operated taxi companies agreed to provide its service to boycotters for their usual 10 cents bus fare— well below the usual taxi minimum. Leaflets describing the boycott were distributed and, fortunately for the protestors, the Montgomery *Advertiser* further publicized the event as it detailed the plans in its front page story.

The King's were eating breakfast Monday morning as the first bus of the day pulled up to the bus stop located in front of their house. They were elated to see that it was empty. The next one was empty as well. King drove around the city for over an hour that morning to view the busses. He was happy to see that virtually all of the busses were void of black riders. Instead of riding the busses to work, they walked, rode bicycles, carpooled and one man even rode a buggy pulled by a team of horses. Leaders expected the Monday boycott to receive 60 percent cooperation, but they were overwhelmed by the near 100 percent support of the black community.

That evening a mass meeting was called to let the people decide whether or not to continue the boycott. There was a huge traffic jam surrounding the Holt Street Church an hour before the meeting was to begin. The 4000 blacks in attendance were evidence of the community's will to continue the protest. King was scheduled to speak but he faced a difficult situation: he needed to rally the community to continue its action, but he had to prevent it from acting in violence. King addressed the massive crowd, and the thousands outside by loudspeaker, asking each person to support the protest enthusiastically but in a nonviolent manner. Said King:

> One of the great glories of democracy is the right to protest . . .
> (but while) these organizations (the Ku Klux Klan) are protesting for

the perpetuation of injustice in the community, we are protesting for the birth of justice in the community. Their methods lead to violence and lawlessness. But in our protest there will be no cross burnings. No white person will taken from his home by a hooded Negro mob and brutally murdered. There will be no threats and intimidation. We will be guided by the highest principles of law and order.

Our method will be that of persuasion, not coercion. We will only say to the people, "Let your conscience be your guide" . . . our actions must be guided by the deepest principles of our Christian faith. Love must be our regulating ideal. Once again we must hear the words of Jesus echoing across the centuries, "Love your enemies, bless them that curse you, and pray for them that despitefully use you." If we fail to do this our protest will end up as a meaningless drama on the stage of history, and its memory will be shrouded with the ugly garments of shame. In spite of the mistreatment that we have confronted we must not become bitter, and end up by hating our white brothers. As Booker T. Washington said, "Let no man pull you so low as to make you hate him."

If you will protest courageously, and yet with dignity and Christian love, when the history books are written in future generations, the historians will have to pause and say, "There lived a great people—a black people—who injected new meaning and dignity into the veins of civilization." This is our challenge and our overwhelming responsibility.

On the same day, Parks was convicted for disobeying the Montgomery segregation ordinance. Leaders of the black community realized that the ultimate success of their protest would require organization and administration from one central control. The Montgomery Improvement Association (MIA) was founded that night; Martin Luther King, Jr. was chosen as its president. King was a relative newcomer to Montgomery but he had gained the respect of the city's black civic leaders. There was never any doubt about his ability; all were impressed with the young reverend's education, background and personality. Since he had not been in the city long enough to become affiliated with any of the factions, all supported King for the MIA presidency. He would prove to be an excellent choice. Importantly, Coretta was also supportive of her husband. Although his acceptance of the position would result in less time together for the couple, she told Martin, "You know that whatever you do, you have my backing." At its first meeting, the MIA declared the boycott would continue until the city met three requirements: 1. Courteous treatment by the bus operators was guaranteed; 2. Passengers were to be seated on a first-come, first-served basis—blacks seated from the back to the front and whites seated from front to back; and 3. The city should employ black drivers on predominantly black routes.

Later that week, the city won a victory as it passed an ordinance making it illegal for the taxi companies to charge less than the city minimum fare of 45 cents. This left the MIA with a large problem. Taxis were now too expensive, busses were boycotted and very few blacks were affluent enough to afford cars of their own. The MIA decided to start a carpool service that would transport the boycotters to and from their workplaces. Montgomery was a large town with a population in excess of 150,000, and finding enough drivers and coordinating the most efficient routes was a major logistical problem for the MIA. King remembered that a similar bus boycott had achieved success in Baton Rouge, Louisiana. He called his friend Reverend Theodore Jemison, who led the boycott, and received many helpful suggestions. Because money was also needed to pay for gas and administrative expenses, the MIA was carrying a heavy financial burden—expenses were approaching $5,000 a month. Many whites in Montgomery and throughout Alabama were also supportive of King and the boycott. The MIA received many donations and letters of encouragement from their "white friends." Black business owners and the numerous black churches donated as much money and resources as they could afford, and the boycott proceeded with amazing support and efficiency. The Montgomery black community was making a statement that they were not happy, satisfied with or willing to tolerate the "white supremacy" doctrine that segregation advanced.

The MIA met with city officials to discuss the situation and the terms under which the boycott would terminate. King and the black leadership found the city unwilling to negotiate on the MIA's three demands. Montgomery mayor, W. A. Gayle and the other two city commissioners took a solid stand that nothing could be done because it would violate the segregation laws. Furthermore, a representative of the Montgomery White Citizen's Council had been invited to the negotiations. The WCC had branches throughout the South with the purpose of promoting segregation. Martin Luther King, Jr. immediately voiced his opposition to the presence of a member of an organization that was openly "anti-negro." The city seized the opportunity to split the MIA's negotiating committee by implying that without King a settlement could be reached. Members of the city's negotiating team unloaded on King, calling him a "stumbling block" and accusing his "closed mind" of preventing a solution. Reverend Ralph Abernathy of the First Baptist Church, countered the attack. He said that King was the spokesman for the group, and the MIA committee and the entire black community were 100 percent supportive of their leader. This gave King the confidence and peace of mind to continue his course of action. The city never was interested in agreement—once Abernathy dispelled the belief that the MIA leadership could be split, the city terminated the negotiations.

Disappointed, the boycott opponents then attempted to end the protest by causing dissention within the black community. Leaflets were distributed and news articles written portraying King and the other leaders as "fat cats" who were needlessly prolonging the boycott because the protest was making them rich. Other public messages to black leaders said that if any one of them challenged this young "upstart" and assumed the leadership that the situation would change immediately and an agreement could be reached. These sabotage attempts had no affect on the unified and determined boycotters, but they did bother King. As the leader of the protest, he was the oppositions primary target and these attempts took their toll on King's mental health. He was not so swayed much by the arguments, but he was afraid they might persuade his colleagues.

After a few days and sleepless nights, King called a meeting of the MIA where he offered his resignation. It was unanimously rejected.

About this time, a letter from a white lady appeared in the Montgomery *Advertiser* in which she described the similarities between the boycotters' methods and those employed by Mohandas Gandhi. This comparison gave the nonviolent approach of King and the boycott a new understanding: the nonviolent methods, at times difficult to rationalize and adhere to, were considered to be capable of achieving success.

Because blacks comprised over 75 percent of the bus ridership, the boycott was having a substantial financial impact on the city and many of its businesses. In response, mayor Gayle, announced a "get tough" policy to deal with the boycott. The carpoolers were harrassed more often and police issued traffic tickets for even the slightest violations. Many drivers feared that they would lose their licenses. While driving one of the routes, King was arrested for driving 30 MPH in a 25 MPH zone. When blacks learned of his jailing, they flocked *en masse* to the jail house. He was not well-treated by the authorities, but upon seeing the growing crowd, they graciously decided to let King sign his own bond. This event had a profound affect on the movement. Because King proved that he was willing to sacrifice in the same way he was asking others to, he and the cause were viewed with increased credibility. The support of the community also gave King the strength and encouragement he needed.

King was tested again and again by the strains and pressures of leading a social reform movement in a physically dangerous environment. He and the other leaders had received many threats against themselves, their families and their homes, but to this point there had been little violence. Perhaps King's greatest challenge of the Montgomery protest—and possibly his greatest triumph—came on January 30, 1956. King was interrupted while speaking at the First Baptist Church—he was informed that his house had been bombed. He quickly left to check the safety of Coretta and their daughter.

A dynamite bomb had been thrown onto their front porch. Coretta believed it only to be a brick or rock but moved to the back of the house anyway. Fortunately, their infant daughter, Yolanda (Yoki), had been asleep in the back bedroom and escaped the blast unharmed. King arrived to find a huge crowd of angry blacks armed with a variety of weapons surrounding his home. King pushed his way through the crowd and the line of white police officers who were trying to control the crowd. King was relieved to find his family unhurt. The mayor and police commissioner were present and voiced their concern that the angry mob outside might start a riot.

King emerged onto his front porch and raised his hand for silence. The crowd hushed in anticipation. King's remarks showed an amazing resolve for the continuance of the non-violent methods of the boycott. Said King:

> My wife and baby are all right. Now let's not become panicky. If you have weapons, take them home; if you do not have them, please do not seek to get them. We cannot solve this problem through retaliatory violence. We must meet violence with nonviolence. Remember the words of Jesus: "He who lives by the sword will perish by the sword." We must love our white brothers no matter what they do to us. We must make them know that we love them. . . This is what we must live by. We must meet hate with love. Remember if I am stopped, this movement will not stop, because God is with the movement. Go home with this glowing faith and this radiant assurance.

Later that night, however, King fought with himself as to how he should feel about the bombing of his house. As he laid awake in bed, he became angry realizing that his family could have been killed. He became angrier still as he recalled how the statements by the city officials had created an atmosphere ripe for this type of violence. King managed to quell this mounting anger because he possessed a great understanding of the situation. Rather than becoming bitter and hateful, King was full of *agape* for the city officials. Later King wrote:

I tried to put myself in the position of the three commissioners. I said to myself these men are not bad men. They are misguided. They have fine reputations in the community. In their dealings with white people they are respectable and gentlemanly. They probably think they are right in their methods of dealing with Negroes. They say the things about us and treat us as they do because they have been taught these things. From the cradle to the grave, it is instilled in them that the Negro is inferior. Their parents probably taught them that; the schools they attended taught them that; the books they read, even their churches and ministers, often taught them that; and above all the very concept of segregation teaches them that. The whole cultural tradition under which they have grown—a tradition blighted with more than 250 years of slavery and more than 90 years of segregation—teaches them that Negroes do not deserve certain things. So these men are merely the children of their culture. When they seek to preserve segregation they are seeking to preserve only what their local folkways have taught them was right.

King's speech to the angry crowd displayed a great belief in his methods, cause, followers and self. The effects of his courageous response were twofold. First, the black community was now completely devoted to Dr. King and the movement. His family had narrowly escaped death and he had as much reason to retaliate in violence as any black in Montgomery. His adamant refusal to part with the nonviolent methods of the movement gave both himself and the boycott increased credibility. In essence, he was leading by example: in the face of this public and brutal act of violence—the details of which were known by all--he courageously turned the other cheek. King was not giving in. He would retaliate, but in his own way—through love and understanding. He would retaliate by continuing the boycott and protest in a lawful, moral and appropriate manner. He would not, however, respond through violence. His example of an acceptable reaction to a violent personal attack was important because it made clear that Reverend King practiced what he preached.

The second effect of his response was a result of the event being reported to both national and international audiences. Television, radio, newspaper and magazine correspondents rushed to interview King and report to the world his unique approach to civil rights. In the same way his courageous reaction to the angry prank victim at Crozer won him praise, his bravery and leadership in this critical situation, which could have resulted in tragedy, caught the attention of the nation. Bloodshed through a violent riot would have focused the nation's attention on the violence and away from the injustice the boycott was protesting. Praises of King and the cause were widespread. Donations to help the boycott, eventually totalling $250,000, flooded in from throughout the nation and even from Europe and Asia. King's wise and courageous words in the face of danger awoke the nation to the evils of segregation. It also made the battle lines very clear: the boycotters placed themselves in the role of the loving, the morally right and the oppressed, while the segregationists made themselves appear as the unjust, hating oppressors.

In mid-March, the city invoked an old and obscure law which made illegal the boycotting of a legitimate business. They issued warrants for the arrests of more than 100 of the boycotters with King's name at the top of the list. King was lecturing in Nashville when he learned of the warrant and decided to cut short his stay in Nashville and turn himself in the next day. He stopped in Atlanta to see his family on the way where his father, fearing for his son's safety, pleaded with him not to go back. King, Jr. did not want to go back because it pained him to make his parents worry. It also looked as if this could be the end of the protest. The devoted boycotters had been sacrificing for more than three months and King feared they might grow weary. But returning to Montgomery to face the challenge and danger was something King knew he had to do.

In Montgomery, King met Abernathy, who was already out on bail, at the jail house. King was astounded but elated by the atmosphere—a large crowd of blacks, some of which had turned themselves in and were out on bail, were laughing, joking and enjoying themselves. King expected their spirits to be as low as his due to this new prospect of defeat. Abernathy explained that the boycotters had rushed to the jail gladly giving themselves up and many were even disappointed to learn that they were not included on the city's list. Elated, King entered the jail, was booked, and released on bail. The trial was scheduled to begin March 19.

The defense presented 28 witnesses over the course of the four day trial. Each told stories of how the bus drivers and police officers had robbed them of their money, dignity, self-respect and even lives. Mrs. Stella Brooks related how her husband had paid his fare and was ordered to re-board through the rear entrance. Seeing that the back of the bus was nearly full, he told the driver that he would rather walk if he could have his dime returned. An argument resulted as the driver would not comply with his request. A police officer soon arrived and told Brooks to leave. He said he would not leave without his dime. The argument escalated and the officer shot and killed Brooks.

Mrs. Martha Walker told of her blind husband getting his leg caught as the driver shut the door on him. Despite Mrs. Walker's screams, the bus pulled away dragging Mr. Walker some distance until he was able to get free. Walker reported the incident but the bus company took no action. These and the other stories explained to the packed courtroom how segregation had produced and encouraged the insults, threats and violence toward black riders. This treatment, argued the defense, was the rationale for the boycott.

On the afternoon of March 22, 1956, Judge Eugene Carter pronounced King guilty. He sentenced King to 386 days of hard labor or a $500 fine plus court costs. King's lawyers immediately appealed the decision and he was released on bond while Judge Carter granted continuances in the cases against the other boycotters until King's case was resolved. King later described his thoughts and feelings as he left the courthouse:

> Ordinarily, a person leaving a courtroom with a conviction behind him would wear a somber face. But I left with a smile. I knew that I was a convicted criminal, but I was proud of my crime. It was the

crime of joining my people in a nonviolent protest against injustice. It was the crime of seeking to instill within my people a sense of dignity and self-respect. It was the crime of desiring for my people the unalienable rights of life, liberty and the pursuit of happiness. It was above all the crime of seeking to convince my people that noncooperation with evil is just as much a moral duty as is cooperation with good.

The boycott continued, but so did the violence and torment of the city officials and the White Citizen's Council. The phone threats and hate mail were all too frequent, sometimes numbering 40 a day, but they had become a fact of life for King and the MIA leadership. After four months of carpooling, walking and sacrificing, the boycotters had become unified not only in purpose, but also in spirit. Rather than weaken the blacks' individual and collective wills, the city's actions often increased the boycotters' devotion to their cause. King explained that, "Instead of stopping the movement, the opposition's tactics had only served to give it more momentum, and to draw us closer together. What the opposition failed to see was that our mutual sufferings had wrapped us all in a single garment of destiny. What happened to one happened to all." This reciprocal support system between King and the black community helped give both the confidence and desire to continue.

In May the MIA challenged the Constitutionality of Alabama's segregation laws in the United States Federal District court. Their case was simple: In terms of education, the 1954 *Brown* decision overturned the 1896 *Plessy V. Ferguson* Supreme Court ruling which established the "separate but equal" doctrine. Therefore, the MIA argued, if separate but equal was no longer valid for education, then it should not be valid for other public facilities either, including city busses. The city of Montgomery maintained that if the busses were integrated, then Montgomery would become a racial battleground. The three federal district court justices then had to decide if it was fair to require one person to surrender his or her Constitutional rights to prevent another person from committing a crime.

On June 4, after weeks of deliberation, the court announced its ruling; in a 2-1 decision, the United States Federal District court declared the segregation laws of Alabama unconstitutional. The city immediately filed an appeal in the United States Supreme Court. A major battle had been won giving the boycotters a renewed sense of hope, but it would take weeks or even months to get a ruling on the appeal from the Supreme Court. For all practical purposes, the situation remained the same. The boycott and carpooling efforts continued, the city of Montgomery refused to negotiate or budge, and the threats, violence and hate mail were perpetuated against the protestors.

In August the insurance carriers suddenly decided to stop coverage on the vehicles used in the carpool as the liability insurance was considered to be too great a risk. The collision insurance was not a problem as it was provided through a black-owned company. Although the MIA eventually was able to obtain coverage through Lloyds of London, the cancellation did cause King and the MIA an added amount of work and concern. The boycott continued throughout the summer with the black participation still approaching 100 percent. On October 30, 1956, the city thought it had developed the final solution. It filed in the Montgomery municipal court that the carpool be dissolved because it was a "public nuisance" and an illegal and unlicensed "private enterprise." A hearing was set for November 13.

This appeared to be the end of the carpool as King nor any MIA officers believed they would receive a fair hearing in the court. The night before the hearing, King, once again, was distraught. In a scheduled mass meeting, he had to tell the loyal and devoted protestors that, in all likelihood, the carpool would be outlawed. This would mean that either the boycotters would have to walk to and from work—regardless of distance and conditions, or they would have to admit defeat by riding the segregated busses. In terms of morale, this was the most difficult of the 343 protest days.

King tried to express some optimism in his speech that night, but his words were not enough to melt the mounting feeling of despair. Said King:

> This may well be the darkest hour just before dawn. We have moved all of these months with the daring faith that God was with us in our struggle. The many experiences of days gone by have vindicated that faith in a most unexpected manner. We must go out with the same faith, the same conviction. We must believe that a way will be made out of no way.

The black community of Montgomery greeted November 13, 1956 with feelings of gloom and uncertainty. The hearing proceeded throughout the morning with each side predictably calling witnesses and making arguments. During a recess, however, King noticed an unusual flurry of activity around the city's table. Soon all of the participants for the city left the courtroom for a discussion room outside. King knew something strange was happening. An excited reporter handed King a note. Unexpectedly and without hearing testimony, the United States Supreme Court had ruled—and upheld the U.S. Federal District court decision that Alabama's segregation law was unconstitutional. King later described his thoughts upon reading the note, "At this moment my heart began to throb with an inexpressible joy. The darkest hour of our struggle had indeed proved to be the first hour of victory."

Predictably, the municipal court ruled in favor of the city to outlaw the carpool, but the Supreme Court ruling no longer made the boycott necessary. It would, however, be nearly a month before the Supreme Court mandate would reach Montgomery. The MIA decided to call off the protest immediately but to have blacks refrain from riding the segregated busses until the mandate was received. In the interim, the MIA held meetings and workshops to instruct black riders how to peacefully and nonviolently ride the integrated busses. On December 20, 1956—382 days after it began—the Montgomery bus boycott ended as King, Abernathy and thousands of other black riders happily boarded the integrated busses.

Some of the most brutal and destructive violence did occur after the integration. Some blacks were beaten, black churches and homes were bombed and busses were shot at. When the bus system shut down for a few days in the hope that the violence would cease, King broke down, feeling a terrible guilt for the violence and possible dissolution of the bus system. However, the black community gave their youthful leader overwhelming support and encouragement. The bombings and beatings abruptly stopped after the arrest of seven white Montgomery residents believed responsible for the violence. Although charges against five were dropped and the other two defendants were acquitted, all Montgomery residents realized that integrated busses were going to be a fact of life.

The Montgomery bus boycott is significant to the civil rights movement, American history and the study of leadership for four reasons. First, the victory dealt a major blow to the Jim Crow laws by making illegal the segregation of public transportation throughout the nation. Segregation, however, was still legal—and practiced—in some public facilities and in private enterprise. Montgomery restaurants, theaters, union meetings and even city parks and recreation facilities were still harbors to the degradation and oppression of segregation. But the Supreme Court ruling set a precedent. It was a giant first step in what would be—and continues to be—a long march to end segregation and racial discrimination in the United States. Because of the Montgomery success, any Southern segregation law could be challenged through litigation with a reasonable chance for a victory. Besides the segregationists themselves, the only obstacle remaining--as President John Kennedy and Attorney General Bobby Kennedy tried to remedy— was possessing the vast resources necessary to document and litigate the countless number of cases. Montgomery, though, created the possibility and provided the hope for future successes.

Second, the Montgomery bus boycott elevated Martin Luther King Jr. to a national figure. Dr. King was thrust to the forefront of the movement where he asserted himself as a dignified, rational, moral and credible leader. In King, black Americans had found a leader behind whom they could unite—not only in Montgomery, but throughout the South. The self-confidence and the confidence of others he gained due to the success in Montgomery made him a stronger and more effective leader willing to try and achieve more for the civil rights cause.

The third reason the event was significant was the success of the nonviolent medium. Nonviolence proved to be a relatively quick and effective method for social reform. It was advocacy for change within the system showing faith in the American form of government that the ideals of life, liberty and the pursuit of happiness could be achieved by all citizens. The protest also showed that social change in America could be effected by peace, love and understanding and without violence and revolution. Because of their success and appeal, King and nonviolence became symbols of the civil rights movement.

Fourth and most importantly, Montgomery symbolized the awakening of the black race in America. The victory proved to the nation—and to themselves—that blacks were not, in fact, second class citizens. They announced through their unified action that they were capable of effecting social change and that they were no longer willing to witness or permit their unjust treatment. They realized their power and importance—politically, socially and economically—as a unified block of 18 million citizens. As a result of the Montgomery successes and the constant reminding of their leaders, black Americans began to believe that they too could live the American dream.

The Southern Christian Leadership Conference

The success of the Montgomery movement encouraged King to challenge other segregationist and Jim Crow laws throughout the South. To do this, King realized an organizational structure would be required. He helped establish and organize the Southern Christian Leadership Conference, SCLC, which had the primary goal to aid local organizations and leaders in their protests of racial injustice. Because King was unanimously chosen for the SCLC's leadership, it was committed to social change through nonviolence. As president, King recruited to the SCLC many excellent black clergy, businessmen, professionals and civic leaders including Ralph Abernathy, Andrew Young, Hosea Williams, Wyatt Walker, C. T. Vivian and James Bevel.

The internal structure of the SCLC would make for an interesting study in organizational dynamics. It had a governing board and executive committee, both chaired by King, and various other committees relating to finance, research, recruitment and to specific protest events. In a traditional model, King, president of the organization, would have been bound, somewhat at least, to the ideas and wishes of these bodies. This, however, was not the case. The SCLC has been described as a "benevolent autocracy." In theory, the SCLC had a traditional chain of command and formal policy making bodies, yet in practice, King had the final word. Rarely, however was there any public disagreement with King's plans or policies. Why then, would any energetic, competent and ambitious person desire to join the SCLC—an organization in which very little traditional power rested outside the presidency? The answer lies in King's leadership style.

King, as all the leaders profiled in this book, did not believe that he inherently possessed all the solutions to the problems his organization faced. King, Anthony, Truman, Kennedy, Iacocca and most other successful leaders have repeatedly shown that a leader's success is dependent on his or her ability to design an organization not simply for the execution of decisions, but to create an atmosphere conducive to information exchange and problem solving. This was one of King's many strengths, but perhaps the one characteristic that made the SCLC a success. His background and education in theology and philosophy taught him to enjoy new concepts and ideas. This experience permeated his life and afforded him the greatest benefit of education—a lifelong commitment to learning and understanding. This was an important personal characteristic that marked his leadership style. The progress made by SCLC—and by King—hinged on the fact that he was a constant opinion seeker.

Although he had the power to commit the SCLC to action and policy without any prior discussion, he rarely did so. He would always seek multiple sources of opinion and advice and attempt to understand both the conservative and radical approaches to the situation. The majority of his information came from within the ranks of the SCLC through the boards and committees. At these meetings, King encouraged the free expression and exchange of ideas because he believed the more information he had, the better his perspective of the situation would be. And, as Truman demonstrated, with a well-developed perspective, it was easier to make good decisions. But this open discussion at meetings sometimes led to heated debates and prompted King to quip that the real need for nonviolence was *within* the SCLC. King also sought information and opinion through informal channels. Not only did members of the SCLC feel they could offer King their opinions, he would often make it a point to ask them. Thus, King's approach to leadership gave the movement a feeling of community—that everyone's ideas were important and should be heard. Because members of the SCLC believed they had a voice in the process, a bond of loyalty was formed. This quickly created a healthy pool of talent from which King and the SCLC recruited.

The SCLC under King, however, was not rule by community, but it did have many of the positive attributes, and few of the negative, of a community concept. This departure from a traditional organizational structure led many observers to conclude that it was disorganized and often in disarray. The difficulties that the structure created were relatively few and usually minor. The benefits of the structure, however, were great. Because decision making rested with one person, the organization as a whole could act and react more quickly.

The external structure of the SCLC was designed so that it would not compete with the NAACP for membership. While the NAACP offered individual memberships, King's organization formed loose alliances with local organizations. These groups would become "affiliates" for a nominal fee. Affiliate organizations could seek assistance and advice from the SCLC and they could send five delegates to the annual convention. Furthermore, the NAACP was a national organization with chapters throughout the United States, while the SCLC remained predominantly a regional organization in the South. This non-competitive structure allowed both organizations to contribute to the civil rights cause and made it possible for the groups to occasionally work together.

Much of the work of the SCLC was to assist and advise affiliates in their protests and negotiations with city officials. The nonviolent training it provided to the local participants was a significant contribution to the numerous protests throughout the South. A larger function of the SCLC, however, was to locate cities and communities with conditions ripe for change. Once a target was chosen, the SCLC moved into the city to help on a massive scale. In essence, the SCLC acted as a funnelling organization, concentrating its money, resources and the national attention on various "hot spots" of segregation. This gave the SCLC the opportunity to choose the turf on which it would fight segregation. Importantly, however, King and his staff learned to confer with the local leaders before taking any action or announcing any plans. King realized their importance and relied heavily on them as they were the experts concerning the circumstances. The affiliate leaders understood the situation better than any outsiders could and they knew the personalities of both the protestors and the city officials involved. Only they could explain to King the important local customs, history and nuances of the often complex circumstances. Thus, instead of the affiliates integrating into the SCLC, their efforts were enhanced and amplified by the SCLC's presence and contributions. To be successful, the protest would have to be a cooperative effort between the affiliates and the SCLC.

The benefits of this method were a result of King's popularity. He could stimulate and mobilize people into action like no other civil rights leader of the time. His presence and speeches excited and inspired local black communities to make whatever sacrifices were needed to achieve the goals of the movement. Additionally, the national press followed King virtually everywhere he went. This was crucial in many of the communities, as King and the nonviolent protesters often met violence at the hands of the segregationist establishments. With national correspondents on the scene, the nation was witness to the injustice and brutality segregation advanced. The nation's conscience and cries for justice applied pressure to segregationists and often proved to be a catalyst for change.

By 1961 the SCLC had grown into a powerful force for social reform and justice from the American system. The basic organizational structure had been established, donations and membership dues were being collected and advice and support were being rendered at the request of many affiliates. However, the SCLC had not yet participated *en masse* in a local movement. King and his main group of advisors had traveled the country lecturing and speaking, but they had yet to be challenged on the scale of the Montgomery bus boycott.

In late 1961 their first test was given by the city of Albany, Georgia. In terms of race relations, Albany was a relatively peaceful city as blacks met little resistance to register and vote. But the presence of segregation could not be overlooked. Blacks held no elected offices nor served on the police force, while virtually all public and municipal facilities were segregated. On the surface, all parties seemed to be content with the status quo as both the NAACP and the KKK had weak chapters in the area. In November of 1961, however, three members of the Student Nonviolent Coordinating Committee, SNCC, formed the Albany Movement. At its first meeting Charles Sherrod, Cordell Reagon and Charles Jones established three modest goals to begin desegregation of Albany: fair employment policies, an end to the Albany police brutality, and the desegregation of the bus and train stations and all municipal facilities. The Albany Movement forwarded these requirements to the city, while it held demonstrations to show its resolve.

On November 22, Albany police chief Laurie Pritchett politely arrested five black protestors at the bus terminal. Pritchett realized that if he charged them with violating the segregation laws, the Albany Movement would have a test case with which to challenge the law's Constitutionality. Instead he arrested them on non-racial grounds such as loitering, disorderly conduct, blocking the streets, etc. This proved to be an effective method for diffusing nonviolent protest.

On December 10 a trainload of "freedom riders" arrived in Albany to challenge the segregation laws. Pritchett arrested them and again booked them on non-racial charges. On the day of the trial, 265 protestors were arrested as they marched to city hall. Pritchett had another ace up his sleeve: he knew the protest strategy was to overcrowd the city and county jails. Therefore, he made arrangements with neighboring cities and counties to use their facilities to accommodate a large number of arrests.

The city had shown signs of a willingness to negotiate and meetings had sparked hope that an agreement could be reached. The Albany Movement president, Dr. William G. Anderson, called his friend Ralph Abernathy to invite King to address a mass meeting. King spoke to a crowd of a thousand the next evening, December 14, in Albany. King, Abernathy and Anderson were arrested the next day for leading a protest. While they were in jail, the Albany Movement and the city agreed to a truce with three provisions. First, all demonstrators would be released from jail. Second, the city would comply with the federal regulations banning segregated bus and train facilities. And finally, a bi-racial committee would be established—after a cooling off period of thirty consecutive days without protest—to further study and address the racial issue.

However, with King and Anderson both in jail, the Albany Movement was not sure who was in charge. Members of the NAACP, SNCC, SCLC and the Albany Movement all laid their claims which weakened the protest. The Albany Movement believed the presence of King and the SCLC would apply adequate pressure to the city to make it agree to more concessions. King had a great impact on the situation in Albany but not in the manner anyone expected. The Albany Movement's confidence was artificially boosted by King's presence which led to a crucial strategical blunder. Its mistake was to stiffen their demands and issue an ultimatum to the city on the verge of the settlement. Enraged by the ultimatum, Albany Mayor Asa Kelley rescinded the truce agreement and broke off negotiations.

Although King, Abernathy and Anderson were eventually released on bail, this blunder led many black activists to soften their approach to the protest. Quarrels again erupted as to who was and who should have been in charge which plunged the entire protest into chaos. King left Albany for Atlanta to keep fundraising and speaking engagements and to call an informal meeting of his staff and the SCLC board members. King was eager to determine what had caused the failure so that his organization would not make similar mistakes in the future. The SCLC realized that entering the Albany situation when the two sides were so close to an agreement was a major folly. It is unclear whether or not King and Abernathy were fully briefed on the progression of the negotiations, but regardless, they learned a valuable lesson.

In July, King and Abernathy returned to Albany to receive sentencing on their previous arrests. Both were sentenced to 45 days in jail or $178 in fines. To make a dramatic statement and rally the black community of Albany, both chose to serve the jail time. The situation between the Albany Movement and the city had reached a stalemate. Neither side was willing to budge in what was becoming a war of attrition. King's defiance to pay the fine and go to jail spurred a new hope for the floundering protest. The excitement was soon crushed as an unidentified man, reportedly black, paid King and Abernathy's fines which meant they had to leave jail. Further dampening the morale of the protest was a federal court ruling that granted the city an injunction to ban further marches. King and the Albany Movement now had to decide whether or not to continue the demonstrations and risk violating the federal order. To the dismay of SNCC officials, King decided not to defy the court. The federal courts had been the only avenue for justice for the civil rights movement and King could not justify violating this order while applauding the favorable ones. He would protest again in Albany only in the event of a successful appeal. Some members of SNCC and the Albany Movement were openly critical of King's decision, accusing him of "chickening out."

The primary reason the Albany protests failed was the calculated moves of Pritchett and the city. Pritchett confronted the nonviolent protestors with nonviolence. He was polite and lawful rather than encouraging or participating in violent reprisals. Additionally, his preemptive measures to secure jail space helped slow the momentum of the movement. Pritchett's nonviolent methods prevented King and the Albany Movement to elevate their protests from unlawful conduct to a broader national appeal for racial justice. In fact, as later events would prove, the federal government would not intervene in the regional conflicts unless violence occurred. King and the SCLC learned these lessons the hard way, but they would not be forgotten. King realized his organization would have to choose its targets more carefully and enter the protests with a plan of action. The failure also made King aware that strong, unified local organizations would be necessary for future protests. Albany was an important test of King's resiliency. It was the first major protest for the SCLC and it ended in a failure. King had watched in frustration as his efforts made little positive impact. He had spent several days in jail, been berated by white segregationists and criticized by local black leaders. King was able to learn and rebound from the experience to achieve success in the next SCLC effort—Birmingham.

In contrast to Albany, Birmingham, Alabama was a city with a rich tradition of violent opposition to desegregation. Leading this opposition since the 1930s was Commissioner of Public Safety, Eugene "Bull" Connor. Connor was a devout segregationist who ruled his city with an iron fist. The SCLC would face a formidable opponent in Connor, who clashed with the powerful labor movement and the Congress of Industrial Organizations (CIO) in the 30s. After World War II, Connor lost a reelection bid to an opponent with moderate views and retired. But in 1956 Birmingham residents called him out of retirement and elected him to his former office.

Opponents of segregation also had a strong presence in Birmingham. Since moving to the city in 1953, Fred Shuttlesworth, black minister of the Bethel Baptist Church, had tried to organize and motivate the black community of Birmingham to protest the segregation laws and practices of Birmingham. To speed this process, he founded the Alabama Christian Movement for Human Rights, ACMHR, in 1956. Shuttlesworth was familiar with the risks and dangers of leading civil rights protests; his house and churched had both been bombed and he had been beaten and jailed for challenging segregation in Birmingham. The ACMHR had steadily grown in strength since its inception, and by 1962 it had a core membership of more than 600 and had become one of the SCLC's most active affiliates.

In March of 1962, students at Birmingham's Miles College staged a boycott of downtown stores, vowing to continue until the merchants desegregated their facilities. It is important to note that contemporary shopping malls scattered throughout the suburbs were non-existent in the 1950s and 1960s. In most cities and towns, the downtown stores were the primary source of economic and daytime social activity. A boycott of those stores could mean hard times not only for the merchants themselves, but also for the municipality in lost tax revenues. By October, merchants, still unwilling to comply, were hurting financially. Some had even seen their amount of business cut in half. Shuttlesworth perceived this to be an excellent opportunity to escalate the boycott and continue it through the Christmas shopping season. Shuttlesworth made arrangements with the SCLC to aid the Birmingham protest believing that a strong unified push would result in victory. The SCLC had three reasons to mobilize in Birmingham. First, the local black community wanted action. Second, the Albany mistakes were still fresh in the minds of SCLC members and Birmingham would be a good opportunity to erase those doubts and move forward. Third, all believed that a victory was possible in Birmingham. However, before the SCLC could mobilize, merchants caved in and five stores desegregated their facilities. Shuttlesworth was ecstatic and advised King that outside help would no longer be necessary.

The victory was short-lived. A few weeks later Connor threatened to prosecute the merchants under segregation laws if they did not restore the separate facilities. This brief reprieve, however, made it impossible for the SCLC to shift gears quickly enough to plan and organize a protest before the holiday season began. King and Shuttlesworth agreed to have the SCLC target the Easter shopping season for protest. Still stinging from the Albany failure, this would give King and the SCLC the necessary time to plan and organize a massive effort.

The SCLC and ACMHR had another major factor to consider as they planned the boycott and protests. Birmingham residents, concerned that Commissioner Connor had too much power, passed a referendum changing the structure of the city government from the centralized commissioner format to a mayor-council charter. The referendum also stated that elections for the office would be held in early 1963 as opposed to the scheduled 1965 date. Three candidates filed for inclusion on the election ballot. On election day, none of the three candidates won a majority, and a run-off was slated for April 2 between the top two finishers, Connor and Albert Boutwell. Boutwell and Connor had very similar attitudes toward segregation; Boutwell was characterized as a "Dignified Connor" while Connor was described as an "Undignified Boutwell." Perceiving little difference, King and Shuttlesworth planned to protest regardless of the outcome.

The election, however, created a problem for King and Shuttlesworth. With a Connor victory, little would change. If Boutwell was victorious, he would undoubtedly ask for a truce with the protestors, demanding a chance to negotiate. The black community was well aware of Boutwell's intentions and motivations but to most observers this would seem to be a legitimate request. A Boutwell victory could mean the indefinite end to or loss of support for the movement. On April 2, Boutwell defeated Connor by nearly 8000 votes in the city election. But Connor sought an injunction in the Alabama Supreme Court to continue in power, contending that he had been elected to serve until 1965 which voided the election. Until the court ruled, Connor was still in control of Birmingham.

The protests began quietly the next day as 20 blacks staged sit-ins in the downtown stores. King expected opposition to the protests from the black middle class but he was surprised by the amount of it. A large number were disturbed and publicly voiced their displeasure with the timing of the SCLC protest. They believed that further demonstrations could prompt the city to rescind the modest gains made by the earlier protests. King was somewhat disheartened by the lack of wide-spread support and the quiet nature of the protest. Connor, to that point, had reacted in a similar nonviolent fashion to Albany's Laurie Pritchett which prevented the movement from gathering any momentum. The lack of support could be blamed on the four month wait to begin the protests. They had been planned three separate times to begin on three different dates and the confusion and frustration was taking its toll on the community's commitment. On Good Friday, April 12, King and Abernathy led a march from the Zion Hill church. They only walked eight blocks toward city hall before Connor had them arrested. This was King's attempt to excite and motivate the Birmingham black community and unify it in protest.

Bull Connor, meanwhile, saw this as an opportunity to break King's spirit. He placed King in solitary confinement and allowed only a few aides brief visits. King's cell was dingy and dimly lit. During these long lonely hours King was engaged in a mental battle to keep his wits. The eight monotonous days King spent in his cell proved to be an excellent example of the redemptive value of nonviolence. King had recently been criticized in a public statement by eight white clergymen for invading Birmingham and leading "untimely" protests. As King sat in his jail cell, he thought about the criticism and how unfounded it was. He began writing a response, first on toilet paper then the margins of a newspaper and finally on a note pad smuggled to him by an aide. The resulting document was of considerable length, but it was a complete and systematic rebuttal to all the criticism both he and the civil rights movement had accrued over the previous nine years. King's *Letter from Birmingham Jail* is a brilliant gemstone in the treasury of American political rhetoric.

In the letter, King provided critics with the rationale behind his presence in Birmingham: "I am here, along with several members of my staff, because we were invited here. I am here because I have organizational ties here. Beyond this, I am in Birmingham because injustice is here." To the issue of timing, he explained that, "We know through painful experience that freedom is never voluntarily given by the oppressor; it must be demanded by the oppressed. Frankly I have never yet engaged in a direct action movement that was 'well timed' according to those who have not suffered unduly from the disease of segregation." King's masterpiece also countered one of the opposition's largest criticisms: "One may well ask, 'How can you advocate breaking some laws and obeying others?' The answer is found in the fact that there are two types of laws: There *just* laws and there are *unjust* laws. One has not only a legal but a moral responsibility to obey just laws. Conversely, one has a moral responsibility to disobey unjust laws." King's document was filled with Biblical and philosophical references while he described the suffering and injustice segregation had forced on his oppressed race for more than three and a half centuries. This time in solitary, although unpleasant, afforded King the opportunity to write a detailed response; his normal work days were far too long and demanding to contain the time or spare the energy to summarize his perspective of the civil rights movement.

King and Abernathy's bonds were posted and they were released from jail on April 20 while their trials were set for the 26th. So far, Connor had responded nonviolently to all of the protests which was having a dulling effect on the movement. Even King's arrest and jailing had only a moderately positive affect. On their day in court, King and Abernathy were pronounced guilty and each received a $50 fine and five days in jail. The court further softened this light sentence by allowing each twenty days to appeal the decision. This soft-line approach prevented King from becoming a martyr, which could have sparked a new excitement in the black community.

On May 2, however, the movement was to forever change. James Bevel, acting for King as he had left Birmingham on SCLC business, organized a march of 6000 school children. Nearly a thousand were arrested by police. This tactic of using children drew sharp criticism but it did provide the spark the leadership was looking for. The next day a similar march was planned starting from the Sixteenth Street Church, but Bull Connor's policemen arrived at the church as the march was commencing. Connor had reached his boiling point. With news reporters and photographers present, Connor's men charged into the crowd of children swinging their billy clubs. Police dogs were turned loose on the now frightened demonstrators. Firemen blasted the children, ages six to 18, with their water hoses which exerted enough force to rip the bark off trees. It was a full scale riot in all respects but one: The protestors had been expertly trained by the SCLC in nonviolence and, with a few exceptions, did not fight back. It was a field day for the press. Although some reporters were beaten and a number of cameras were smashed, they were witnessing the product of two of America's greatest tragedies: segregation and racial prejudice. The nightly news and morning papers had lengthy stories describing the violence and chilling photos of police dogs attacking demonstrators. One infamous photo pictured five police officers holding a woman to the ground as she was beaten. Because the violence and abuse was capsulized by the reporters, the nation was quickly and graphically awakened to the brutality and injustice of segregation. The next three days witnessed similar events but included a growing aptness for the demonstrators to violently retaliate. May 6 and 7 were the two most violent days--on both sides. Bricks, rocks and bottles were hurled at police officers as they were no longer ordered by Connor to contain the protest, but to drive the demonstrators back to the black part of the city. By this time, the city's jail facilities were overwhelmed; more than 2000 protestors had been arrested while thousands more waited for their turn.

Incredibly, it looked as if the situation would grow worse. Protest leaders feared they might not be able to prevent their demonstrators from retaliating in violence. Furthermore, Commissioner Connor asked for and received five hundred state troopers from Alabama Governor George Wallace to help "restore order." Negotiations had been fruitless as neither side was willing to budge. President Kennedy sent Burk Marshall, the assistant attorney general to Birmingham to help negotiate a settlement. Both John and Bobby Kennedy had made public statements calling for an end to the violence and they made numerous phone calls to participants on both sides appealing for restraint, but their efforts were to no avail. All realized that a confrontation between demonstrators and Connor's reinforced squad would result in unprecedented bloodshed. Fortunately, the Kennedys were able to delay the protests for a few hours, and in the deep shadow of what could have been a national tragedy, a truce was declared ending the protest.

The terms of the agreement included the desegregation of the downtown stores' facilities and the establishment of a bi-racial committee within two weeks to further study and advise the mayor on racial issues. The agreement, however, did not accommodate all of the demonstrators demands. Although all demonstrators were to be released from jail, King received criticism for accepting the term that the charges against them would not be dropped. This would mean that bail money would have to be raised for each jailed demonstrator. King was fairly certain, however, and may have received assurances that the federal courts would nullify the segregation and anti-protest statutes that most of the demonstrators had been charged with. The federal courts did in fact rule in that manner, which meant that bail money was refunded and their cases were, in effect, dismissed.

Birmingham was a turning point in the civil rights movement. It was the handwriting on the wall for the South that segregation's days were numbered. It was also a reminder to the nation that freeing itself from segregation was not and would not be an easy task. Additionally, it gave the SCLC and King a much needed shot of confidence, and it made the nation graphically aware of the injustice of segregation. The public outcry and demand for change resulting from the Birmingham protests were responsible for the introduction, and possibly the passage, of the 1964 Civil Rights Act. King's determination and leadership were more than just a catalyst in the successful Birmingham movement.

The Birmingham success in the Spring of 1963 was followed by a late summer march on Washington D.C. to lobby Congress to pass Kennedy's Civil Rights Act. On the hot afternoon of August 28, King delivered one of America's greatest oratories to 200,000 people from the steps of the Lincoln Memorial. The thoughts, hopes and ideas of his *I Have a Dream* speech are still pursued by most Americans of all colors and creeds today.

In 1965, a protest similar to the one in Birmingham was staged by the SCLC in Selma, Alabama. A freedom march was planned to start in Selma and cover a fifty mile stretch of highway to Montgomery. At the Alabama State Capitol, they would hold a mass rally, appealing to Governor Wallace and the legislature for their support of desegregation measures. King arrived in Selma and attempted to check-in at the Albert Hotel which had been built more than a hundred years prior by slave labor. As he was waiting at the front desk, a white man approached King and punched him in the face. As King recoiled, the man kicked him twice in the groin. The man was arrested, but the incident was indicative the treatment segregationists would afford blacks throughout the Selma campaign. Selma Police Chief Jim Clark and his police force reacted more violently than even Bull Connor's. Police dogs, water cannons and billy clubs were again the standard weapons used against the demonstrators. Broken bones, cuts and bruises were the norm for the participants, and one young black was shot and killed during a night protest as he tried to stop police officers from beating his mother. In the same way Birmingham was responsible for the 1964 Civil Rights Act, the violence in Selma resulted in the 1965 Voting Rights Act.

The civil rights movement was the ultimate test of will for its leaders. The physical abuse, harsh criticism from both whites and blacks and the violent opposition and degradation of segregationists were a heavy burden for King—or any person—to manage. King had the added burden of responsibility. In many instances he felt personally responsible for the pain, suffering and death inflicted on his followers that were a result of the protests he led. King was able to win the mental battle and stay determined. His resilient character provided the strength not only for himself, but also for his followers and for the movement.

There are those that argue that King was just at the right place at the right time, and that the movement made him rather than him making the movement. Although there is some validity to the issue of timing, King's strict adherence to nonviolence kept the social and emotional forces of the civil rights movement relatively peaceful and prevented what could have evolved into the bloodiest and most divisive conflict on American soil since the Civil War. King made the ultimate sacrifice for the cause he believed in. The oppressive forces of segregation ended his life, but his message, determination and dream still live in the hearts and minds of all people who cherish and desire freedom and justice.

*   *   *

We must learn from the great thinkers and leaders of history and King was perhaps this century's greatest. His tenacity and resilient character, like that of Susan B. Anthony, illustrate that no task is too great or too difficult if it is rooted in justice and is undertaken for the common good of society. As did John Kennedy, King had a vision which gave Americans hope. Their unique and ideal images of the future inspired a generation to create a nation and a world free of terror, poverty and misery and full of peace, understanding and equality. Although humanity has made great strides since their deaths, we have a good distance to cover before we can consider their goals accomplished. Each of us, however, must learn from their examples of leadership to help society re-define our national priorities and create a national vision.

The United States and the world cannot forget Dr. King, but each of us will remember him in our own personal way. Two months before he was assassinated, Dr. King expressed to his Ebenezer Baptist Church congregation the way in which he would like to be remembered:

Every now and then I think about my own death, and I think about my own funeral. And I don't think of it in a morbid sense. Every now and then I ask myself, "What is it that I would want said?" And I leave the word to you this morning.

If any of you are around when I have to meet my day, I don't want a long funeral. And if you get somebody to deliver the eulogy, tell them not to talk too long. Every now and then I wonder what I want them to say. Tell them not to mention that I have a Nobel Peace Prize, that isn't important. Tell them not to mention that I have three or four hundred other awards, that's not important. Tell him not to mention where I went to school.

I'd like somebody to mention that day, that Martin Luther King, Jr., tried to give his life serving others. I'd like for somebody to say that day, that Martin Luther King, Jr., tried to love somebody. I want you to say that day, that I tried to be right on the war question. I want you to be able to say that day, that I did try to feed the hungry. I want you to be able to say that day, that I did try, in my life, to clothe those who were naked. I want you to say, on that day, that I did try to visit those in prison. I want you say that I tried to love and serve humanity.

Yes, if you want to say that I was a drum major, say that I was a drum major for justice; say that I was a drum major for peace; I was a drum major for righteousness. And of all the other shallow things that will not matter. I won't have any money to leave behind. I won't have the fine and luxurious things of life to leave behind. But I just want to leave a committed life behind.

The Challenge

Despite the great leadership of these five remarkable Americans at critical periods of history, the United States still faces a present crisis. Not only do we witness few examples of good leadership, but social problems are many and ominous, and procrastination leads to disaster. We face an uphill struggle, but the incline is not so steep that we cannot eventually reach the summit. Clearly, America faces a great challenge. This challenge is to produce enough strong and effective leaders to permeate all levels of American society and to help them to solve the multitude of problems. First, however, it is important to review the differences and commonalties between these five great leaders as we begin the national search for leadership.

These extraordinary five were a very diverse group. Their amount of education was varied; King had a Ph.D., Iacocca a Masters Degree, Kennedy and Anthony earned Bachelor Degrees, while Truman excelled with only a high school diploma. Kennedy, Anthony and Iacocca were born and raised in the Northeast; King grew up in the South; and except the 18 years he spent in the Senate and White House, Truman lived his 88 years in Independence, Missouri. Only Kennedy was born into a wealthy family, and Iacocca was the only one to amass a personal fortune during his career. Two were president of the United States, two led civil rights movements and one found his calling in the automobile business. The previous three generations of only the King and Anthony families lived in the United States—the families of the others were recent immigrants. Kennedy was an Irish-Catholic, Truman had a Methodist and a Baptist for parents, Iacocca was an Italian Catholic, Anthony was a Quaker and King was a Southern Baptist. These differences illustrate the loss society bears when it permits the existence of prejudice and discrimination of any kind on any basis—political affiliation, age, race or gender.

Kennedy, Truman and King were Democrats while Anthony and Iacocca changed their political affiliation several times throughout their lives. Despite what some politicians affirm, leadership is not bound by political affiliation. If Democrats had the leadership market cornered, the United States would not have experienced the lifelong brilliance of Abraham Lincoln or Teddy Roosevelt. To a lesser degree, Republicans Dwight Eisenhower, Gerald Ford and Richard Nixon exercised good leadership at certain times in their careers. However, if only Republicans were privy to the secrets of leadership, Franklin Roosevelt, Woodrow Wilson and Robert Kennedy would not have influenced American society. Furthermore, there are leaders whose political affiliation is not common knowledge. Former NFL Commissioner Pete Rozelle, basketball star Magic Johnson, entertainer Bill Cosby, and journalist Walter Cronkite have long been recognized as leaders in their respective fields.

Another important difference is age. The five leaders hit their primes at vastly different ages. King was the youngest at 27, while Anthony, the eldest, continued her activism and leadership from her mid-30s through her mid-80s. Had she retired at age 65, women might not have been granted the right to vote as early (or late) as 1920. Truman was not elected to the Senate until he was 48, and he ended his political career at age 66. Kennedy was elected to Congress at age 29 and reached his pinnacle at 43. Iacocca enjoyed his many major successes between the ages of 40 and 60. The diversity of their ages demonstrates that intellect, desire, life experience, natural ability and even fate have a greater bearing on leadership ability than does age.

Although racism, sexism and discrimination still exist and equal opportunity is not yet a reality, great strides have been made within the last generation. Women and minorities have asserted their importance and proven their abilities. As we move toward the twenty-first century, more and more opportunities are available to these groups. The successes and accomplishments of Democratic

National Chairman, Ron Brown; Reverend Jesse Jackson; Los Angeles Raider football coach, Art Shell; Representative Ben Nighthorse Campbell, and former mayor of Denver Federico Pena prove that leadership is not bound by race. The victories and triumphs of Texas Governor, Ann Richards; author/activist Gloria Steinem; Congresswoman Pat Schroeder; former vice presidential candidate, Geraldine Ferraro and journalists Jane Pauley and Barbara Walters prove that leadership is also not gender-bound.

All Americans need to realize that the problems we face are extremely diverse and complex. As John Kennedy wrote in his 1963 book, *A Nation of Immigrants*, "Perhaps our brightest hope for the future lies in the lessons of the past. The people who have come to this country have made America, in the words of one perceptive writer, 'a heterogeneous race but a homogeneous nation'" Indeed, people of every race, creed and of both genders, with their unique perspectives, diverse abilities and original ideas are America's greatest strength. We cannot afford to waste any talent. What we must do is focus our attention on the specific components of a person's personality, character and method of operation that makes him or her a good leader.

In this respect, the commonalties that exist between these five are particularly revealing. All looked to themselves to make things happen rather than complain that someone else was not initiating the action. All were goal oriented and, to different degrees, self-motivated. All believed in the need to break from the status quo. They believed that an integral part of human nature is the inherent desire for improvement. The improvement of one's self and situation unleashes the human spirit, strength and creativity that reveals endless possibilities. This attitude and commitment to progress generated many enemies for each. As a result, two of the five were assassinated and it was attempted on a third. While they understood the meaning and importance of the past, they did not dwell on it—they focused on the future and moved forward.

Furthermore, all dealt with failure at different points throughout their careers. Each was intelligent, resilient and learned from mistakes—both their own and those of others. All were willing and able to do what was necessary—both pleasant and unpleasant—to get the job done.   All five were good communicators and some were good public speakers.   All were excellent listeners, were open to new ideas and sought information and advice from a variety of sources. Most had a good sense of humor—in general, situationally and concerning themselves. And, perhaps most important, all enjoyed what they were doing. These similarities illustrate that leadership ability is based on personality, character and one's methods of operation—not basic demographics.

Not one of the leaders could consider all five characteristics—vision, integrity, resiliency, communication and decisiveness—as a strength. Anthony excelled at resiliency and integrity, Truman at decisiveness and integrity and King was resilient and a master communicator. Kennedy was a great communicator and was resilient in that he learned from his mistakes while Iacocca was decisive and resilient. The one characteristic, however, that they had in common which sets them apart from other managers, leaders and public figures is a vision. They were not, however, equally visionary; they possessed the trait to varying degrees.

Iacocca was working within a relatively inflexible and highly structured system. In the automobile industry, the scale by which success is judged is well-defined—profitability. Within these narrow boundaries, Iacocca was successful and visionary. He had ideal and unique images of products that would out-price, outsell and outperform the competition and have great appeal to the consumer. But the structure of the auto industry confined Iacocca much more than the systems affecting the other four leaders profiled. This inaccurately makes Iacocca's vision seem to be less developed than the others'. Rather it was relevant, and thus, appealed to a much smaller audience. What makes Iacocca great is that he excelled to the limits of his chosen system.

Anthony had a strong vision, but was required to spend a great deal of time in a managerial capacity. Truman had similar forces affecting his vision. Because he was virtually in a perpetual crisis, he had less time to construct and develop a vision. Although he was forced to spend a large portion of time in a damage control mode, his vision of a free and healthy Europe and peace without a third world war were realized.

Kennedy and King were the most successful visionary public figures the United States has produced since the Second Constitutional Convention. Many were visionary before and since these two great leaders, but shortfalls in the other four characteristics prevented their success. All five illustrate one vital and absolute axiom: long-term positive change is not possible without a vision.

The public's perception and attitude toward leaders and leadership greatly affects the quality of leadership in our society. Leaders, and especially politicians, are viewed with a certain skepticism. As reports of failures, mistakes and corruption surface, the public's confidence fades. The news media rushes to expose and judge these events but it fails its reciprocal duty to positively reinforce good examples of leadership. Although editors and news directors often deem them "un-newsworthy," publicizing and encouraging these positive people, events and personal characteristics forges a greater understanding and provides a merited boost of confidence in our leaders. This is of vital importance to the creation of a leadership literate society.

America has had a rich tradition in leadership and it is imperative that we maintain these traditions. But this great challenge we face does not permit us the luxury of time or resources for leaders to cultivate themselves. America must actively produce its leaders. To answer this challenge, let us put politics, bigotry and prior differences aside and work together—black, white, Asian, native American, Hispanic, male and female—as a cohesive unit to create and realize one ideal and unique image of the future—a leadership literate society.

Index

A

Abernathy, Ralph, 171, 183, 187, 190, 194, 199, 200
Acheson, Dean, 72, 75, 77
Alabama Christian Movement for Human Rights (ACMHR), 196-98
Alcoa, 55-57
Anderson, Rudolph Jr., 133
Anderson, William G., 194
Anthony, Daniel, 12-13
Anthony, Guelma, 12
Anthony, Lucy Reed, 12-13
Anthony, Susan B., 10, 11-44, 136, 145, 149, 171-74, 190, 206-10
Armstrong, Neil, 98
Asabranner, Brent, 105
Atlee, Clement, 68-69, 71
atomic bomb, 63-66

B

Baker, James, 77
Batista, Fulgencio, 116
Bay of Pigs, 106, 115-125, 128, 134
Beecham, Charlie, 138
Beecher, Henry Ward, 41, 42
Bennis, Warren, 5, 139
Bergmoser, Paul, 152
Bevel, James, 190, 200
Black Muslims, 168-70
Bloomer, Amelia, 18
Boutwell, Albert, 198
Bradley, Omar, 78
Breakers Hotel, 58-59
Brooks, Stella, 184
Brown, Edmund, 112
Brown, Ron, 207-08
Brown Vs. Board of Education of Topeka, 98, 175
Bundy, McGeorge, 127
Burke, Arleigh, 123
Bush, George, 77
Butts, George, 152

C

Cady, Stanton, Elizabeth, 13, 14, 17, 18, 28-30, 35, 38-40, 41, 42
Caldwell, Phil, 146
Campbell, Ben Nighthorse, 208
Carter, Eugene, 184
Carter, Jimmy, 109
Castro, Fidel, 116-22
Central Intelligence Agency (CIA), 116-123, 124
Chrysler Corporation, 37, 140, 148-158
Churchill, Winston, 64, 65, 67-68, 71
Civil War, 21-28, 51, 52, 98, 171
Clark, Jim, 203
Congress of Industrial Organizations (CIO), 196
Connor, Eugene "Bull", 196, 198-201, 203
Cosby, Bill, 207
Cronkite, Walter, 207
Crowley, Richard, 33
Cuban Missile Crisis, 116, 126-135
Custer, George A., 116

D

Dauch, Dick, 152
Declaration of Independence, 14, 25, 98
Declaration of Sentiments, 14
De Gaulle, Charles, 67
Dewey, Thomas, 48
Dexter Street Baptist Church, 163
Dobrynin, Anatoly, 126
Douglass, Frederick, 14
Dulles, Allen, 123, 124

E

Ebenezer Baptist Church, 159, 204
Eisenhower, Dwight, 78, 91, 92, 94, 95, 96, 98, 102, 109, 112, 116-17, 122, 207

F

Fairlaine Committee, 141,143
Ferraro, Geraldine, 208
Fillmore, Millard, 33
Fitzgerald, John F., 88
Fomin, Alexander, 132-33
Ford, Bill, 146
Ford, Gerald, 207
Ford, Henry II, 144-47
Ford Motor Company, 37, 136, 137, 139-48, 158

G

Gandhi, Mohandas K., 161, 173, 174, 180
Gayle, W.A., 179
General Motors, 37, 140, 152
Greeley, Horace, 17, 27
Greenwald, Gerry, 151
Gromyko, Andrei, 127-28

H

Harriman, Averell, 79
Hart, Gary, 42
Himmler, Heinrich, 67
Hirsch, E.D., 4, 5
Hiss, Alger, 93
Hitler, Adolph, 67
Humphrey, Hubert, 91
Hunt, Ward, 33

I

Iacocca, Lee, 10, 136-58, 171, 190, 206-10
Iacocca, Lia, 147
Iacocca, Mary, McCleary, 138, 147-48
Iacocca, Nicola, 136

J

Jackson, Andrew, 13
Jackson, Jesse, 208
Jefferson, Thomas, 14
Jemison, Theodore, 178

Jim Crow laws, 171
Johnson, Ervin "Magic", 207
Johnson, Lyndon, 91, 96, 102, 112-13, 127, 135
Jones, Jesse Jr., 56

K

Kai-shek, Chaing, 79
Kefauver, Estes, 91
Kelley, Asa, 194-95
Kennedy, Jacqueline Bouvier "Jackie", 90, 109
Kennedy, John F., 10, 43-44, 88-135, 136, 164, 166, 167, 188, 202, 206-10
Kennedy, John F. Jr., 109
Kennedy, Joseph P. Jr., 88-89
Kennedy, Joseph P. Sr. "Joe", 89
Kennedy, Patrick Joseph, 88
Kennedy, Rose Fitzgerald, 88
Kennedy, Robert F., 123, 125, 127, 128, 134, 188, 202, 207,
Kennedy, Theodore "Ted", 88
Khrushchev, Nikita, 93, 103, 126, 127, 129, 130, 131-33, 134
King, Alberta, 159
King, Alfred Daniel, 159
King, Christine, 159
King, Coretta Scott, 162, 178, 180
King, Martin Luther Jr., 10, 110, 136, 159-205, 206-10
King, Martin Luther Sr., 159, 183
King, Yolanda "Yoki", 181
Klu Klux Klan, 160, 170, 193
Kouzes, James, 5, 6
Krock, Arthur, 112

L

Laux, Gar, 151
Lenud, Philip, 162
Lincoln, Abraham, 39, 51, 84, 207
Lodge, Henry Cabot Jr., 90, 93

M

MacArthur, Douglas, 73-75, 78, 79-85, 87